This is one of the finest relationship books ~~...~~ Holly and Philip Wagner are a delightfully authentic couple who made me laugh, think, rethink and put into practice their excellent ideas. Their writing and communication style is fresh, spontaneous and extremely practical. I highly recommend this book.

Dr. Jim Burns, Ph.D.
President of HomeWord, Author, *Creating an Intimate Marriage* and
Closer: Devotions to Draw Couples Closer Together

I am so excited that you have this book in your hands. Philip and Holly are not only one of the best teaching couples on relationships, but they also work hard to live out the principles outlined in this book. You will find practical tools to help you go higher in every level of your relationships, and you will laugh as you learn from their own journey. I highly welcome and recommend this great book.

Christine and Nick Caine
Author, Speakers and Founders of A21

Real, raw and straight shootin'! Holly and Philip do not hold back! What a great book to teach from. I plan on using this at our church and, if I can remember to do so, I'll give proper credit to the authors . . . lol!

Ted Cunningham
Coauthor, *From Anger to Intimacy*, *As Long as We Both Shall Live* and *The Language of Sex*

Philip and Holly Wagner have a teaching style unlike any other—they live and teach out of a dynamic relationship with both God and each other. Philip and Holly are dear friends of ours, and their perspective on healthy relationships and maintaining a fun, God-centered marriage is refreshing. Their humorous writing style and passion for people will captivate your mind and challenge your heart as we all seek for God's leading in this important area of life.

Brian and Bobbie Houston
Senior Pastors, Hillsong Church, Australia

We all want it—the fairytale ending "they lived happily ever after"—yet most of us don't know how to get it. Philip and Holly Wagner know how to help. Their honest and humorous approach to the desire of all our hearts is a practical and personal how-to that we all desperately need.

Robert and Debbie Morris
Senior Pastor and Executive Pastor, Gateway Church, Dallas, Texas
Bestselling Author, *The Blessed Life*

Relationships can be a tangled web of heartache if not navigated with precaution and care. From the nerve-wracking first date to the covenanted walk down the aisle, men and women have to take time to lean in, listen carefully, learn and make wise decisions. Pastors Phillip and Holly have given the body of Christ a gift—not just with this book but also with their lives. Their own marriage has mentored and encouraged many others—including my own. What they have penned in these pages is a must-read for everyone who wants to reap a maximum harvest in his or her relationship.

Priscilla Shirer
Bible Teacher and Author

I have been teaching the differences between men and women since the 1970s. This book is so refreshing in how it honors those differences. Thank you, Holly and Philip, for being real and sharing your life on every page.

Gary Smalley
Bestselling Author, *From Anger to Intimacy, As Long as We Both Shall Live* and *The Language of Sex*

When we dream of the perfect relationship, we often imagine the trust, excitement and security of a lifelong commitment. In reality, we know that a truly successful relationship takes work, dedication and a willingness to humble ourselves and learn. In this book, our good friends Philip and Holly Wagner spotlight the journey that successful relationships must experience—a journey that they have been travelling themselves for more than 25 years. Whether you are single, dating or have been married for decades, throughout these pages you will encounter more than relational advice or quick fixes. Instead, you will discover the scriptural truths that will help reawaken you to God's desire for your life and your relationship.

Ed and Lisa Young
Pastor and Ministry Leader, Fellowship Church, Grapevine, Texas
Co-authors, *The Creative Marriage* and *The Marriage Mirror*

loveworks

develop healthy relationships in a "love broken" world

Philip+Holly Wagner

LEAD PASTORS OF OASIS CHURCH

Regal

For more information and
special offers from Regal Books, email us at
subscribe@regalbooks.com

Published by Regal
From Gospel Light
Ventura, California, U.S.A.
www.regalbooks.com
Printed in the U.S.A.

Library of Congress Control Number: 2014934289

ISBN 978-0-8307-7030-4

Rights for publishing this book outside the U.S.A. or in non-English languages are
administered by Gospel Light Worldwide, an international not-for-profit ministry.
For additional information, please visit www.glww.org, email info@glww.org, or write to
Gospel Light Worldwide, 1957 Eastman Avenue, Ventura, CA 93003, U.S.A.

Dedicated to all of you who are committed to doing
the work required to have an amazing relationship.

Contents

Introduction

I don't think I actually "fell in love" with Philip.

It was more like growing in love.

I just remember my heart beating harder when I was with him.

I remember wanting to spend every moment with him.

I remember loving him as I played his newly recorded album (on LP and cassette, not CD—we are old).

I remember being inspired by his relationship with God. His faith seemed so easy and so real.

I loved (and still love) listening to him teach. He made (and still makes) the Bible seem practical and relevant.

I loved (and still love) how compassionate, patient and non-judgmental he was (and still is) with people.

I loved (and still love) how he made (and still makes) me laugh. No one makes me laugh the way he does. Of course, no one makes me as mad as he does either!

I know Philip far better now than I did when we first began our journey together. And I love him more. He and I have learned how to value and honor each other. We have gotten better and better at communicating in a way that builds each other up. We have learned how to appreciate the areas in which we are different. We have learned patience. We have realized that together we are stronger than we would be alone.

Those things said, there have been moments along our journey when my husband has driven me nuts, when I have questioned my choice of husband.

"Remind me that divorce is expensive and that murder is against the law," is a plea I made to a friend a number of years ago. I laugh about that comment now, but back then I wasn't kidding! At that time, our marriage wasn't fun, maintaining it was so much work, and Philip didn't "understand me"!

Perhaps you have felt this way at times. You vaguely remember those lovin' feelings—you're just not having them now.

Well, take heart. You are not alone.

Or maybe you are single, and you don't really want to be.

Maybe your friends are getting married, and you are debating whether or not you should just settle for someone. You are wondering if there is someone out there for you.

Well, yes—there is.

But you might just have to do some work.

On you.

And on what you are looking for. Yeah, there are still great men and women out there. But there are some you shouldn't touch with a 10-foot pole. Hopefully this book can help you tell the difference between them.

Our modern society encourages our need for independence and individualism, and at the same time it recognizes the hunger in all of us for real relationships. But you will not have the relationship of your dreams if you focus on yourself and your needs. Recently, a person sitting next to me on an airplane asked me what I thought the biggest problem in marriage was. Hands down, I responded, it is selfishness. I want what I want, and I want it now. I want to be loved without ever really doing the work of loving.

After almost 30 years of building a marriage, of navigating some of the tricky curves, Philip and I want to share a little of what we have learned.

One of the last prayers Jesus prayed was that we, the Body of Christ, would become one (see John 17:20-23). Sounds a lot easier than it is! If we, the Body of Christ, are going to become one, it will probably start in our homes.

One definition of the word "extreme" is "farthest removed from ordinary or average."

I like that.

You and I need to be *extreme* people in just about every area of our lives. And certainly in our relationships! *Average* marriages are failing at an alarming rate. So how about if we become *extreme* in our commitment to build our marriages? How about if we become *extreme* in our determination to understand more than to be understood?

So much of our lives are spent navigating the ever-tricky road of relationships. And some of us (not you, of course!) have made very stupid decisions when it comes to the people we have let into our hearts. While we may never become experts on the whole relationship thing, I do think we could all get a little better at it.

That is the heart of this book.

Our hope and prayer are that it helps you.

Love works.

Love takes work, and love does work.

So here we go!

Philip and I will alternate chapters. And on some subjects, you will hear from both of us, just with different perspectives. Philip's chapters will definitely be more organized.

This shouldn't be a surprise!

Introduction

Beast: That hurts.
Belle: If you'd hold still it wouldn't hurt so much.
Beast: If you hadn't run away, this wouldn't have happened.
Belle: If you didn't frighten me, I wouldn't have run away.
Beast: You shouldn't have been in the West Wing.
Belle: You should learn to control your anger.
Belle: By the way, thank you for saving my life.
Beast: You're welcome.
Beauty and the Beast, Disney

Love is powerful. We are created to enjoy love, to love and to be loved.

We don't function well without love. Love is heaven's gift to all of us.

We humans have a way of mishandling the gifts given to us. Many people today are doubtful about love, wanting to keep their distance. Many, many people are weary of love.

My wife Holly is a gift to me. When I first met her, I was love-struck—smitten. We were so in love. Later in our marriage I was still smitten, only in a different way completely. I could not see how she was actually a gift—I mean, we were and are so different.

When she's hot, I'm cold; when I'm too warm, she's too cold.

She wants to go faster; I'm thinking I want to slow things down a minute. She doesn't just walk to the beat of a different drummer; sometimes she's listening to a different song altogether.

You say *tomato,* I say *to-mah-to.* She says potato, I say—hash browns.

Holly and I see most things differently. We used to try to change each other. We both got so frustrated. This almost killed our marriage.

But we finally figured it out. We are a team. Now, 29 years after joining forces, we recognize that our individual strengths bring strength to our team. Team Wagner. Her strengths enhance our relationship. My strengths enrich us.

A major change in our relationship occurred when we started to recognize our differences, accept them and find a way to respect each other and actually admire those differences. Except when the thermostat is set at 65 degrees in the summer. You will read a lot about that in this book.

Among our differences is the way we view "time."

Take the "five-minute issue," for instance. When we are getting ready to go out for the evening, it takes me 10 to 12 minutes; if I'm taking a shower, 15 minutes. Holly needs a lot more time (which is not the issue).

Here is where the problem starts: I'm more literal, while she is more metaphorical. I like to be on time, which to me means 5 to 10 minutes early. Holly takes "on time" with a more philosophical interpretation.

"Holly, are you ready to go?"

"I'm ready," she says.

I think she means that she's ready *now*, so I go out and start the car. But she doesn't really mean that she is ready to go now— like *right* now. Her *now* is in more like, say, five minutes-ish. So why doesn't she just say "in about five minutes"? Even if she said five minutes instead of now, she wouldn't mean five *actual* minutes.

It's more general than that.

I get frustrated.

Then she reminds me, "Five minutes. You know, like the five minutes you tell me are left in the basketball game. Which is more like 15 or 20."

"Oh. Right. Good point."

However, now, 29 years later—I'm the one who is usually late.

In marriage, keeping your eye on the big picture, on the vision for your life, is crucial. This will help you navigate through many battles—large and small. When you don't do this, it's easy to get stuck on little issues that can destroy your relationship or at least put the fire out that got you to marry each other in the first place.

Ladies, you are not going to understand everything about men. Men, you are not going to understand everything about your wives.

Take "the chewing issue." We are sitting in bed reading at the end of the night. My wife is snacking. She is eating some kind of chips. It is the loudest noise I've heard all day.

"Excuse me, do you think you can chew more quietly?"

"I'm just chewing. There's no volume on chewing," she defends.

"How can that much noise"—I suddenly realize I'm heading into dangerous waters—"come out of such a cute jaw? I'm not criticizing, I'm just saying."

"Just read. Stop picking on me."

"Sorry."

She reads a few more minutes, closes her book and turns out her lamp.

"Are you going to read much longer?" she asks. "Because the light bothers me."

"I'm reading Grisham; just a couple more chapters," I say. "Does the light bother you?"

"Of course it bothers me."

I think about saying, *I would have already read them, but I was distracted with the chewing.*

But I manage to resist—this time.

And then she says a couple sentences that are too quiet for me to hear.

"What?"

She now repeats what she said, only at a lower volume.

"Are you mumbling, or did you have something you wanted to say?"

"Goodnight, Philip."

"So—I guess there will be no sex tonight, then?"

I try to stop the words before they come out of my mouth, but—too late.

We both lay there staring up at the ceiling, thinking, *God, help me understand this person lying next to me.*

Driving in silence is another common experience among married people, especially when you are trying to figure out, *Who am I married to?* and *What just happened?*

It's a strange thing, but Holly and I find ourselves asking those same questions sometimes—even after all these years.

We can let these little annoying conflicts define who we are and our relationship, or we can keep a greater purpose and vision in mind— like unity, love and changing the world.

Look at this Scripture:

May your fountain [*the life of your soul*] be blessed, and may you rejoice in the wife of your youth. A loving doe, a graceful deer—may her breasts satisfy you always, may you ever be intoxicated with her love (Prov. 5:18-19).

Don't you love the Bible?! I don't understand every Scripture, but as a husband, I've really tried to get a grasp on this one. But let's not focus on the breast part right now. We'll address that in the last chapter.

The *New King James Version* of verse 18 translates this idea of being intoxicated as, "Always be *enraptured* with her love" (emphasis added).

Anyway, this is God's desire for your marriage—for you to be enraptured with each other's love, or, to say it another way, to be enraptured with the love of your spouse.

There are some important secrets to having the kind of love that is as full of passion and life as it promises to be. There are some secrets to keeping love alive and fresh. They are not big secrets, really. Sometimes we just aren't paying attention.

Women flourish when the men in their world love them— truly love them. When they are honored and empowered by the men in their life to pursue their dreams, they can reveal an even deeper beauty.

Men flourish when the women in their life love them. When men feel admired, respected and supported, they can have a deeper value in family, a greater confidence in becoming the men they were created to be. It is then that they have the potential to achieve more of the things that really matter in life.

Men often don't realize the impact they have on a woman's soul.

Dads underestimate their imprint on their daughters.

Brothers underestimate their influence on their sisters.

Boyfriends are often oblivious to the mark that will remain on the soul of the girls they date.

And husbands don't realize the importance of their touch on the heart of their wives.

I read one time that a woman's skin is ten times more sensitive to touch than a man's skin. That means ten times more sensitive to a cold touch, a warm touch, a selfish or embracing touch, a harmful touch, a non-sexual touch or a sensual touch. This touch we are talking about can be physical, emotional or verbal.

> 'Twas not into my ear you whispered
> But into my heart
> 'Twas not my lips you kissed
> But my soul.[1]

Women often do not realize that their genuine and effective expression of respect and honor to the man in their life inspires him to become the man of their dreams.

Yes, love works. It works very well.

I was thinking about what Jesus said when his own hometown dismissed the significance of His teaching and His power: A prophet without honor can do no mighty works—especially in his home (see Mark 6:1-6).

What a tragedy. Think of a man who can go anywhere and be honored, but when he comes home, there is very little honor available. Men often avoid home for this very reason. Men are drawn to people because of how they feel about themselves when they are with those people. Attract or repel. It's in your words.

In this book we will look at how men and women, despite our varying idiosyncrasies, can work together to build a love life that brings fulfillment, joy and passion to both parties.

Reading this book will hopefully help you understand a little more about the person you love.

Men are different from women. Men are not the enemy of women; they are just different. Now I don't represent *all* men. I'm not the spokesman for the entire team here. I'm just one man, one voice trying to explain, trying to bridge the gap between women and the men they love—and who want them to love you back.

Women are different from men. They have a beauty waiting to be revealed. This beauty requires the fertile ground of adoration, security and a well-planned touch.

Hopefully after you read this book, you will understand the opposite sex more, maybe laugh a bit more and enjoy relationships a little more. The better we understand each other, the less likely we are to look at each other and think, *What is wrong with you?* or *Who is this person I married?*

No matter what condition your relationship is in—whether you have been happily married for 10 or 15 years or are a newlywed or have already experienced a divorce—I believe that *love works*!

Really! It's the most powerful force in the universe.

Love can change the heart of a man or a woman.

Love can heal the deepest wounds.

Love can ignite the dreams of your heart.

Love works! Love never fails.

Love works! When we think love is *not* working—it is.

Love works! When we think that love is futile, it's probably not love that we are evaluating.

Look at one of the most famous portions of Scripture ever:

Love is patient, love is kind. It does not envy, it does not boast, it is not proud. It does not dishonor others, it is not self-seeking, it is not easily angered, it keeps no record of wrongs. Love does not delight in evil but rejoices with the truth. It always protects, always trusts, always hopes, always perseveres. Love never fails (1 Cor. 13:4-8).

Love is powerful, fulfilling and worth every bit of the work it takes.

Someone told me that men don't often read relationship books. Hey guys, let me tell you something: *If you will do what others will not do, you can have what others will not have.*

You may read this line a few times in this book.

But let me say again, my brotha, that I believe that this book will help you gain understanding that will bring strength to both your life and to your marriage.

Let's get on with the excitement.

1

Mirror, Mirror, on the Wall

Holly

It is your moral obligation to be happy.

Dr. Laura Schlessinger,
The Proper Care and Feeding of Marriage

I praise you, for I am fearfully and
wonderfully made.

Psalm 139:14, *ESV*

It is not your spouse's job to give you a life. It is not his or her job to make you feel good about yourself.

Jesus told us that we are to love our neighbors as we love ourselves (see Luke 10:27). Maybe we do—and that's the problem.

We may not really love who we are, so we may not be that great at loving anyone else. And loving people is why we are here. You and I are supposed to be the human expression of God's love to this very hurting world. We will never be able to do that if we don't love ourselves.

There are some big reasons why we must love ourselves.

One of the biggest is that it's very hard for others to love the real us when we're trying to be someone else.

We all need to grow and make changes. When dating, however, we need to be careful that we don't try to change who we really are. I have overheard dating couples having conversations that go something like this:

"Do you like to travel?"
"Oh yes, I really like to travel." (I know she hates it.)
"Do you like Thai food?"
"Yes, I love it." (Again, I know that he doesn't like it.)
"I really love classical music."
"Me too." (No, she doesn't. She is lying. She is seriously into country.)

They are setting the other person up.

Why? Because they are not comfortable with who they are and are trying, instead, to be who the other person might want. That gets confusing.

Julia Roberts's character in *Runaway Bride* has this problem. She doesn't really like herself, so she tries to be whoever the man she is dating wants her to be. She doesn't even know how she likes her eggs; she eats them cooked however the man she is with prefers them. Not good. It's only after she takes a little time to figure herself out that she is ready to commit to a marriage.

Just be yourself.

There are plenty of people who will think you are wonderful. Be who you are.

Don't waste your time, or another person's, by setting him or her up.

Another reason we must love ourselves is that if we don't, we will choose unhealthy people to marry. We are more likely to settle for less, even accepting mistreatment, because we feel we don't deserve better.

You are a child of the King! You have the right to aim high when choosing a date or a spouse—but you won't if you don't love yourself.

That said, let's keep a level head. Brace yourself. There is no perfect guy or girl out there. Movies and fairy tales spoil us, but we have to learn to navigate the reality of our human nature in light of God's best for us. We are all on a journey, so if you are waiting for Mr. or Ms. Perfect, forget it.

But you don't have to accept Mr. or Ms. Way-Below-Average either.

Nope.

Let people grow up first.

I like being around people who are confident.

Not arrogant.

Arrogance is unattractive and ugly and is often a mask for insecurity.

But quiet confidence is great.

Someone who can laugh at himself or herself and can take a joke without getting offended is worth waiting for.

Do the Math

When you like who you are, you're not overly needy.

It is hard to build intimacy with someone who is needy. Needy people are exhausting. And they make very bad choices in relationships.

There was a pop song by Mariah Carey on the radio every five minutes not too long ago. The lyrics moan something like, "If I can't have you, then I don't even want to live!"[1]

It sounds so tragically romantic to say that losing your lover or your lover's affection would make life unlivable.

But it is not healthy.

I can live without Philip. I don't want to, because I love doing life with him. And he and I are planning on growing old together. But because I know who I am and like who I am, the truth is— I could live without him. This makes me not a needy person. I don't look to Philip to give me a purpose to live.

God calls all of us to be interdependent on each other. By definition, that means "mutually dependent." No one is an island. When we are unmarried, we are interdependent on our friends. Not trying to live an isolated life. When we marry our interdependence begins to include our spouse. We should engage in reciprocal relationship with our mate and reserve our total dependence for God alone. Only God can be our everything, because He alone is perfect. He gives us purpose, destiny and a reason to live. My husband is not perfect, so I look to God for my purpose to live, not to Philip. Leaning totally on our husband or wife is too much pressure for our spouse to handle. We are not designed to carry that kind of load.

We are created for partnership.

In the movie *Jerry Maguire*, Tom Cruise's character says to the love of his life, "You complete me." Now that certainly sounds romantic, and we probably all sighed when we heard it. But honestly, that is nonsense.

We shouldn't be looking for someone to complete us.

You are not some fragmented person looking for a spouse to fill the gaps. God didn't create you as a half. A healthy relationship is when two wholes come together. The goal is for you and me to be wholes.

When God told Adam that it wasn't good for him to be alone (see Gen. 2:18), He created the woman, Eve, as Adam's partner. She was not created to be a drain for him to dump on.

Solomon said that two are better than one (see Eccles. 4:9).

Doing the math, that means that $1 + 1 = 2$

By way of contrast, $\frac{1}{2} + \frac{1}{2} = 1$ which is less than 2. One is the same number God started with, which means that a "partnership" of two halves will not further the purpose of heaven on Earth the way two whole persons coming together can. The purpose of marriage is to glorify God, to be the example of love between Him and His church (see Eph. 5:32). Two whole people can engage in a mutually dependent relationship with honest, open and vulnerable communication and accountability while encouraging and urging each other further and deeper into the purpose of God.

Two halves united together typically experience false intimacy, veins of co-dependency, secrets, hiding, miscommunication and fear about each other's purpose and destiny. It is hard to encourage your mate to become who he or she is in God when you aren't sure who you are in Him.

My ability to like myself does not come from me thinking that I am so wonderful but from God thinking it (see Ps. 139:14). I am God's masterpiece, His one-of-a-kind creation (see Eph. 2:10). And honestly, the deepest needs of my soul are met by my God. I have an honest and real relationship with my Creator. I do not expect Philip to meet needs that only God can.

Now I am not saying that you don't have needs that your spouse is supposed to meet. Men actually like to meet a woman's needs. Philip often helps me fix things. (I don't mean he fixes things around the house, because he doesn't. If it takes more than a hammer or WD-40, we have to call someone.) But he helps me when I need to clarify a teaching message or negotiate the emotions involved in girlfriend-ship or organize my sometimes-scattered thoughts. There were a few times as I navigated my breast cancer battle that he helped me conquer fear, reminding me what God says about healing. When I needed reassurance, he gave it. When I needed someone to hold me in the doctor's office, he did.

And he needs me. To find things. To encourage him. To introduce him to new people. To play. Together Philip and I have accomplished far more than either of us could have alone.

I am not saying that we don't have legitimate needs. We all do, and our spouse can meet them. But having needs and being needy are two different things. And that is the point I am trying to make.

Neediness demands. Having needs asks.

Independent—not good.

Dependent—not good.

Interdependent—*good*.

When we don't like who we are, then we are constantly looking for someone else to fill us up. And while Philip can certainly be an encourager—as he should be—he is not responsible for how I see myself.

There might be a lot of reasons for our insecurity—past abuse, neglect, rejection or abandonment. All of us, to one degree or another, have experienced at least one of these. Nevertheless, at some point we must begin to believe that we are who God says we are—and to live our lives out of that knowledge.

Insecure men tend to be negative and critical. They can't laugh at themselves and are often just mean or manipulative. For both men and women, the only way out of insecurity is to see ourselves as God sees us. When we begin that journey, we bring strength, kindness and love to our relationship.

I heard someone say once, "If I get hit by a truck, it's not my fault; but it will be my responsibility to learn to walk again." We have to face our past, our issues, our hurts and wounds if we desire to be a great mate. We have to take responsibility—not the blame, but the responsibility to heal, grow and change into a healthy individual rooted in God's love and in His Word.

Who Are You?

There are about five billion of us on the planet who believe in God. That's good. But we need to take that belief one step further and not only believe in God but also that He created us for a purpose.

You are not an accident.

No matter what your parents told you, you were put on the planet at this time in history for a specific reason. God plucked you out of eternity and entrusted you with this time in history.

He could have chosen any time for you to be born, but He chose now.

There must be a reason. You have a purpose and a destiny to live out.

And we really won't know our purpose if we don't know our Creator.

If I want to know specifics about my Prius, I don't ask another car. I ask the company that made the car. I have had to read the manual a few times as I have learned all about my new hybrid.

The first step toward liking yourself is knowing that you were created for a purpose and that it is a good one.

Knowing that you are a child of the King changes everything. Really knowing that we are loved and accepted by God changes everything! You can learn God's ways and mature into loving His character as you realize that the sum of your human experience is not who God is. In other words, God is not who your earthly father was, who your abuser was, who your backbiting, critical exes were. That is not His character. His character is good.

The next step to liking yourself is to discover who God is, who you are in Him and what your purpose is. You can get to know your Creator and His plan for you by reading His manual. The Word of God, the Bible, is His letter to you, His instruction manual for you. It's not a rulebook with impossible standards that you can never live up to; it's an expression of love that communicates and propels you forward into God's very best.

Another reason that we must know who we are is so that we can determine what we'll do. We can't figure out what we're going to do in life backward. I can't rely on what I do to determine who I am, because if what I do is snatched away, or if I fail at it, then I'll see myself as a loser. LeBron James is an amazing basketball player, but what happens when he can no longer play? What about the Julia Robertses and Luciano Pavarottis of the world? What happens when they can no longer do what they do? Will they be confused or depressed? Will they take it out on their loved ones?

What about you?

Is your identity wrapped up in what you do?

Before you were a wife, mother, teacher or lawyer, you were a loved-beyond-measure, perfectly created daughter of the King. Before you were a husband, father, engineer or doctor, you were a loved and blessed son of the King.

We don't get our identity from our driver's license. Most of the stuff on there is wrong. I certainly don't weigh what it says I weigh! And I actually think my address has changed!

We don't get our identity from our passport (that only tells us where we have been).

We don't get our identity from school report cards (many of us might still be dealing with some negative stuff teachers said!).

We don't get our identity from a mirror.

You and I get our identity from our Creator. It is through God's eyes that we get a true picture of the individuals we are.

Here is some of what our amazing God has to say about us. All we have to do is believe it. Maybe saying it out loud will help:

- I am a child of God (see 1 John 3:1).
- I am a joint-heir with Christ (see Rom. 8:17).
- I am called (see Jer. 1:5).
- I am purposed (see Eph. 2:10).
- I am chosen (see Eph. 1:11).
- I am fearfully and wonderfully made (see Ps. 139:13-14).
- I am equipped for battle (see Eph. 6:10-17).
- I am more than a conqueror (see Rom. 8:37).
- I am a part of God's plan for justice on the earth (see Isa. 61:1).

- I am the righteousness of God in Christ (see 2 Cor. 5:21).
- I am free from condemnation (see Rom. 8:1).
- I am the temple of the Holy Spirit (see 1 Cor. 6:19).
- I am free from sickness and disease (see Matt. 8:17).
- I am delivered from sin (see Rom. 6:7; John 3:16).
- I am accepted in Him (see Eph. 1:5-7).
- I am loved (see John 17:23).
- I am complete in Him (see Col. 2:10).
- I am a new creation in Christ Jesus (see 2 Cor. 5:17).
- I am delivered from the power of darkness and translated into God's kingdom (see Col. 1:13).
- I am adopted by God (see Rom. 8:15).
- I am training the next generation to live well (see Titus 2:3-5).
- I am an ambassador for Christ (see 2 Cor. 5:20).
- I am saved by grace (see Eph. 2:8-9).
- I am created to bring glory to God (see 2 Cor. 3:18; Col. 1:15-17).
- I am living to honor and worship God (see Rom. 12:1).
- I am transformed by the renewing of my mind (see Rom. 12:2).
- I am redeemed from the curse of the law (see Gal. 3:13).
- I am in Christ (see 1 Cor. 1:30; Col. 3:3).
- I am the will of God (see Jas. 1:18; Rev. 4:11).

Seeing ourselves as God sees us is a primary step on the journey of loving ourselves. I am completely loved, completely accepted, completely forgiven and complete in Him. I am the will of God.

Set a Goal and Go for It!

There are some other steps we can take on this journey.

Setting a goal and overcoming all the obstacles on the way to reaching it will do great things for how we see ourselves. Not only does it feel great to meet a goal we have set, but meeting our goals is also a great way to build endurance—and to learn a little word called "tenacity." It takes a proactive, do-whatever-it-takes attitude to meet a goal.

During my 30 years as a pastor, I have talked with many young men and women who have struggled with this issue of identity. Change for them has begun with starting to see themselves through God's eyes. Change has continued with setting a goal and reaching it.

I talk to many young people with various addictions—sex, drugs, food, shopping. They see themselves as failures.

And as long as they do, they will never be free.

But once they see themselves as loved by God and reach just one goal, they are well on the way to health.

For some the goal was getting a "sobriety job"—having regular hours, showing up when they were supposed to and being accountable to someone. For others it was finishing school. For some it was taking an exercise class, and showing up every week. For others it was losing 50 pounds.

A weakness of mine was that I didn't always finish the projects I started. I am a great starter—it is just my finishing that needs work! Being weak in this area actually affected how I saw myself. I knew that I needed to start something and finish it. And it needed to be something significant. Something other than finishing reading a book or eating a triple-scoop cone!

At that time in my life I was taking my son, Jordan, to karate class. As I watched the classes, I began to think, *I can do this*. Plus, I noticed that at every level a student passed, a new color of belt was given, all the way to the black belt.

It was like a prize, and I like prizes.

So I signed up for karate.

Perhaps that wasn't the easiest of goals for me to reach, but that was what I did. The first day of class, I showed up in my new white uniform and stiff white belt. I was so excited, because I had seen the movie *Karate Kid*, and I wanted to learn to do the amazing kick from the end of the movie. I just knew it wouldn't be long before I wowed my family and friends with my incredible ability.

Well, we didn't learn that amazing kick the first day. Or even the fortieth day. Bummer!

For months I learned how to fall.

This is not what I had signed up for!

I spent hours learning how to fall to the front, fall on my back, fall to the side. Fall. Get up. Fall. Get up. Fall. Get up.

Boring!

To be completely honest, I wanted to quit. But that had been my pattern for years.

As soon as a project got a little mundane or slightly boring, I would quit, feeling justified—because why should I have to put up with boring? And then I would look for something more exciting.

Here's a tip for free: sometimes life, marriage and work are boring. They become routine. Because we are grown-ups, the decisions we make during those times actually say a lot about our character. Previously, the decisions I made during the boring part of projects revealed that I was a quitter.

But this time I didn't quit.

I kept the goal of a black belt in front of me.

A few years into the karate challenge, my son decided that he wanted to devote most of his time to basketball. He no longer wanted to study karate.

Great.

Now my karate goal became an inconvenience. It wasn't easy to figure out what to do with the rest of the family while I continued to take classes. I almost quit at that point.

Another tip for free: Reaching goals is never convenient.

Three years into my study of karate, it began to get physically difficult for me. The moves I was required to learn were tough. The forms (a series of intricate movements) I had to memorize were so complicated that I wondered if my goal of getting a black belt was too hard for me. Karate is a contact sport, and that was becoming more and more evident—we were sparring by this point in my training, and I ended up with more bruises than I wanted.

Last tip for free: any worthwhile goal is difficult and can be painful to reach.

Four and a half years after I started karate, I passed my black-belt test.

Yippee!

Were there times when it had been boring? Yes.

Were there times it had been inconvenient? Yes.

Were there times when it had seemed too difficult? Yes.

Just the fact that my goal *was* difficult to finish made it even more valuable to me. Getting my black belt did things for the way I saw myself that nothing else had done up to that point.

I had started something.

And finished it.

You can too. Pick something, anything. Find a goal, and begin the process of reaching it, overcoming the obstacles on the way: boredom, inconvenience, difficulty and others. When you finally reach your goal, even through all the bumps and bruises, you will feel amazing! Your confidence will soar as you allow life to extract the potential lying dormant or unknown from inside you. You will realize that there is so much more inside you than you originally thought.

Are you enjoying your life?

I'm sure you have challenging moments, but are you basically happy?

Are you interesting? Or do you bore even yourself?

It is so much easier to be around someone interesting—someone who is passionate about something—*anything*. Do you have a hobby you are invested in or a cause you are fighting for?

(By the way, women, if your biggest interest is in finding or keeping a man, you are not very interesting. And no man will think so either.)

When we like who we are, we engage with the world. We read books. We have interests. We have hobbies. We love life!

Green (with Envy) Isn't Your Color

When people are confident in their purpose and have a healthy self-image, they have no occasion or time for envy. Think about it. Why do we get jealous of others? Usually because we want what they have without paying the cost they paid to have it and because we aren't truly enjoying who we are.

I can't sing. Not one note in key.

I have tried. I have taken lessons. Which is why I am always amazed at those who can really sing.

I also can't draw. Not at all. Stick figures are the extent of my portrait ability. Art classes have not helped. I am in awe of those artists on the street who can draw a portrait in about 10 minutes.

Given these realities, I have a choice. I can be envious of people who can sing and draw, or I can be happy that there are people on the planet to whom God has entrusted those gifts and be thankful for the gifts He's given me.

None of us were created with the exact same purposes, personalities or destinies. Each of us is unique. Each of us needs to spend time discovering who we are and what our purpose is instead of trying to be like someone else and wanting his or her gifts. That will only lead to frustration and envy.

Someone who truly likes himself or herself can rejoice when a friend lands a job, gets married or is offered an amazing opportunity.

God's opportunities are limitless—He has great things in store for you. Just keep walking on the path He has assigned to you, and keep discovering *why* you are there. The doors God plans for you to walk through will not require you to break them down. God will open them for you. You just have to be ready and not distracted by someone else's open door. Get great at celebrating the successes of others at home, at work and in your friendship circle. Life is so much better when our security rests in God.

Many scholars agree that Proverbs chapter 31 was written down by King Solomon but dictated to him by his mother. In many versions of the Bible, this chapter highlights the "virtuous woman." "Virtuous" is a great word. Its root means, in part, "a force on the earth." Women are designed to be a force on the earth.

A force on the earth for good.

We are designed to make a difference.

To be a part of the solution.

And we are designed to be this force before a man even enters the picture. I am not to wait for a man, including my husband, to make me virtuous. The responsibility is in my lap. The challenge for the man, according to that chapter of Proverbs, is to find this woman. To find the virtuous woman. Smart men know how to discover the virtuous woman.

Remember: marriage is a place for two wholes to meet, not a place to get neediness met.

Happiness Is Simple

Part of being comfortable in our own skin is making the decision to be uncomplicated. I got a letter a few years ago from my friend

Bobbie. In it she wrote, "Holly, I just want to be your uncomplicated friend." That got me thinking. And I decided that is the kind of person I want to be: uncomplicated. You know, the kind of person who is exactly what people see. No hidden agenda, no hidden motive. No eggshells to walk on around me. Just uncomplicated.

Isn't it refreshing to be with someone like that? Someone with little or no emotional drama? It is so hard to be with the kind of people who make you think, *I am not sure who they are going to be today.*

I want to be an uncomplicated wife for my husband. Not sure that I always accomplish that, but it is certainly my plan. I want to be the peaceful presence in his life. I don't want to be a problem he has to solve.

Philip and I certainly have our issues to deal with, but I have decided that I don't want to carry the issues all day and have a funky attitude while we are working them out.

There is a story in the Bible about three men. Shadrach, Meshach and Abednego loved God, and in spite of a new law in the country commanding them to bow to an idol, they would not do it. The king did not like their decision, so they were thrown into a fire. Yet they did not get burned up. The king said he saw a fourth man in the furnace, a man who looked like the Son of God. He told the guards to let the three men out, and when they did, the three men's clothes and hair weren't even singed and "there was no smell of fire on them" (Dan. 3:27).

I love that picture.

I wonder how many of us could go through challenging times and not come out looking and smelling burned?

It's tough to be around people who bring their past and all its shackles into every second of every day.

Let's be a little easier and more uncomplicated than that.

I think so much pressure would be relieved in relationships if we just decided to be happy with our circumstances, no matter what they may be, and happy with ourselves. There is no person on the planet that can make us happy; we just have to decide to be.

I have talked to women whose husbands carry grudges. They basically pout for days because something did not go how they wanted it to go. This is not being an uncomplicated spouse. We are all going to make mistakes in marriage. Being a happy and uncomplicated spouse means being quick to forgive and move on. (We will talk more about forgiveness later.)

Abraham Lincoln reportedly once said, "Most people are as happy as they make up their minds to be." I like that. It puts the responsibility in our own lap. Regardless of what is going on in the world, regardless of what is going on in our circumstances, we can control our attitude.

My son, Jordan, has spent some time in sub-Saharan Africa working to see that water wells are built in communities in dire need of fresh, clean water. After one of his trips, he shared this observation: In the midst of absolute, abject poverty, children were running around and laughing. Their circumstances were seemingly horrible. Many of their parents had died from AIDS. They lived in mud huts. They ate maybe once a day. They had no clean water. Yet they were happy.

I am just thinking here, but it seems to me that most of us aren't in circumstances quite that dire. Maybe we can choose to smile.

People sometimes say to me, "Holly, being happy is just your personality. It's easy for you." I don't think so. I roll out of bed in the morning same as you. Like yours, my life is not perfect. I just make a decision. When I see Philip, am I going to put a smile on my face? When I go into the office, what kind of attitude is going with me?

Happiness is not a cloud that descends.

It is not a personality style.

It is a choice.

It is a decision to follow a certain path.

The *Amplified Version* of the Bible often defines "blessed" as "happy, fortunate and to be envied." If we want to be happy, we must do the actions that produce happiness. As Americans, we are promised the rights to life, liberty and the *pursuit* of happiness. Some people have misinterpreted that to mean that we all deserve happiness. No, we don't. We only deserve the opportunity to pursue it.

We find happiness when we make conscious decisions to do what produces it. Let's take a look at a few of the paths that lead to happiness according to the Bible. I encourage you to track down even more paths and get on them. Happiness is within your grasp.

"He who despises his neighbor sins [against God, his fellow-man, and himself], but *happy* (blessed and fortunate) is he who is kind and merciful to the poor" (Prov. 14:21, *AMP*, emphasis added).

Want to be happy? Be kind and merciful to the poor.

"*Happy* (blessed, fortunate, enviable) is the man who finds skillful and godly Wisdom, and the man who gets understanding [drawing it forth from God's Word and life's experiences]" (Prov. 3:13, *AMP*, emphasis added).

Want to be happy? Find wisdom. Get understanding.

"*Happy* (blessed, fortunate, prosperous, to be envied) are the people whose God is the Lord!" (Ps. 144:15, *AMP*, emphasis added).

Want to be happy? Let God be your God.

"Blessed (*happy*, fortunate, prosperous, and enviable) is the man who walks and lives not in the counsel of the ungodly [following their advice, their plans and purposes], nor stands [submissive and inactive] in the path where sinners walk, nor sits down [to relax and rest] where the scornful [and the mockers] gather" (Ps. 1:1, *AMP*, emphasis added).

Want to be happy? Be careful who you spend time with.

"Blessed (*happy*, fortunate, to be envied) is he who has forgiveness of his transgression continually exercised upon him, whose sin is covered" (Ps. 32:1, *AMP*, emphasis added). Want to be happy? Live every day knowing that you are forgiven.

"Blessed (*happy*, fortunate, to be envied) are those who dwell in Your house and Your presence; they will be singing Your praises all the day long" (Ps. 84:4, *AMP*, emphasis added).

Want to be happy? Don't just attend church. Do life there.

Water from Your Well

You and I have a huge role to play in creating the atmosphere of our home. Proverbs 5 basically instructs us to keep focused on our marriage. It includes a warning about being seduced away by the "sweet" words of someone else. Verse 15 challenges spouses to "drink water from [their] own well" (*NLT*).

Now I am aware that most of us don't get our water from a well. We simply turn on a faucet. But in biblical times (as in many communities in developing nations today), water was scarce, and wells were carefully guarded. I have learned through our work building wells with Generosity Water that you can't just stand beside a well and expect water to appear before you. You have to lower a bucket or prime the pump. You have to *do something* to bring the water up.

Proverbs 5:15 is basically saying, "Hey, quit looking at other wells. Look at your own well! Do some work to get the water out of this well."

In contributing to the atmosphere of your home and relationship, how do you drink from your own well? What can you do, what can you say, that will bring fresh water into your home?

What can you do to create a good atmosphere?

How about making a decision to think good thoughts about your spouse, even on days when you want to think bad ones?

Another proverb tells us that as we think in our heart, so we are (see Prov. 23:7). What we think determines where we go—our perception of the world, including our attitude toward our spouse and our measure of love and respect for him or her, by how we think. We control the direction of our thoughts.

We are not puppets. We are not robots. We can control our thoughts.

Maybe not the first one, because sometimes we are bombarded with a thought from out of nowhere. But we can control where we let that thought go. The second thought is ours. We control it.

There have been times when Philip has done something that totally annoyed me. Or maybe he hasn't done something that he said he would do. (Grr . . .) Maybe he got too busy, or he forgot, or he just decided that he didn't want to do it.

I could get irritated or get my feelings hurt. And there are times that I do. If I don't control my thoughts, negative feelings take over.

Or maybe one of my kids said or did something that created more work for me. (Very annoying!) Things like that happen to all of us. But I have noticed that I can either nurse my feelings of irritation until they are magnified, or I can catch my thoughts and stop the avalanche of bad thoughts that only produce destruction.

I am not saying that we shouldn't talk about what is bothering us or discuss issues that are important. It's just that if we don't control the thoughts that come barreling through our mind, then the words that come out of our mouths will not be helpful.

And the apostle James tells us that if we can't keep a tight rein on our words, we deceive ourselves and our religion is worthless (see Jas. 1:26).

This is where liking ourselves comes into play. I have found that those who like themselves tend to be happier, which means they create a better atmosphere wherever they are. If what's happening in our heads and hearts is generally positive, our environment and our relationships will reflect that.

If You Can't Say Something Nice . . .

People who like themselves tend to be freer with compliments. They are not worried that giving a compliment will take anything away from themselves, so they often look for something good to say about someone else. But some people are critical and seem to find fault everywhere they look. The sad thing is that these people are often even more critical of themselves than of others. Not a fun way to be.

How are you at giving compliments to the people in your world? To your spouse? Maybe you should ask your husband or wife.

People who are comfortable in their own skin can laugh at themselves. They don't take everything soooo seriously.

I have fallen off a stage in the middle of a teaching.

I have had wardrobe malfunctions while cameras were rolling.

I have said words that, while appropriate in one culture, are absolutely *not* in another.

I have misspelled words while Twittering to thousands of people.

Embarrassing? Yes. But do I take out that embarrassment on others? No. I just laugh and wonder what will be next.

Go on the journey of loving yourself. It's the first step toward having great relationships: loving our neighbor as ourselves. Get rid of those voices in your head that cause jealousy, strife and insecurity. Read God's Word, and let Him tell you what He thinks of you.

As we learn to love who we are in God, it will bring life and joy to every season of our lives. It will deepen and strengthen our marriages, our communities and ultimately our world.

Think It Through

Women

1. Read Psalm 139. Focus on the phrase "I am fearfully and wonderfully made." Why is it important for us to love ourselves?
2. Are you a whole person? In other words, are you complete in who God made you to be? How might looking to your husband to complete you create pressure on your marriage?
3. A guy is attracted to a girl who has interests of her own. What are some things that you enjoy doing? (Remember, if your primary interest is finding and keeping a guy, that is not interesting!)
4. What does "virtuous" mean? God chose *now* as your time to impact the planet. Read Proverbs 31:10-31. What is God calling you to do with your life, in your family, at your job, as a wife?
5. Go back and read the list of "I ams." Which one stands out most to you? Why? Be tenacious in making that "I am" a truth in your heart that empowers you in living out your life.

Men

1. Whose job is it to make you happy? Why?
2. A healthy relationship is when two whole people come to-gether as one. What happens when you look to your wife to complete you rather than finding your completeness in God?
3. Neediness *demands*. Having needs *asks*. Do you demand that your wife meet your needs, or do you ask her about the things you want? How can you move toward expressing your needs in a way that will bring true intimacy?
4. Read Proverbs 31:10-31. If you are single, are you looking for a virtuous woman? If you are married, how can you help your wife to be the virtuous woman God designed her to be?

5. People who can laugh at themselves are comfortable in their own skin. When is the last time you had a good laugh at yourself? (I fell off a stage, remember?) Try not to take everything *sooo* seriously.

2

Frog Kissing and Princess Rescuing

Philip

You have to kiss an awful lot of frogs
before you find a prince.
Graffiti

Theories pass. The frog remains.
Jean Rostand

You can identify them by their fruit, that is,
by the way they act. Can you pick grapes from thornbushes,
or figs from thistles? A good tree produces good fruit,
and a bad tree produces bad fruit.
Matthew 7:16-17, *NLT*

There is an old fable about a young princess who finds a talking
frog. The frog tries to convince her that if she will kiss him, he will
turn into a handsome prince and then marry her, and they will live
happily ever after.

The princess faces this dilemma: What if the frog is just making
the whole thing up? What if she takes the risk, kisses a slimy and
disgusting frog and then—nothing happens? Then again, what if
the frog is telling the truth? He could be the prince of her dreams!

I guess the purpose of telling a young lady that "you have to kiss some frogs before you find your prince" is to encourage her to keep trusting and opening her heart to people, even after she has experienced a broken heart. Yet acting on this advice, a woman will keep trusting men who are not good potential mates, hoping that if she "kisses" the next one with her kindness and grace, he will become the man she needs.

Could this idea be more wrong? Every one of us experiences some personality enhancement because of the positive impact of someone's love. But *total transformation*? That definitely has "fairy-tale myth" written all over it!

A girl thinks she wants the fairy tale. She is tempted by the fairy tale, but who wants to kiss a frog, really? Even in the story of *Sleeping Beauty*, for instance, what woman in her right mind really wants to fall into a coma and be "kissed awake" by some guy who goes around kissing women in comas? What kind of nut is this guy?

Fairy tales are weird.

Stop kissing frogs! Aim higher!

Men think they want to rescue the damsel in distress. They want to be a beautiful young woman's hero. Why not go for a young woman who does not need to be "rescued" but rather who you can join forces with and change the world.

I want to tell you what I told my own daughter, who is now 22, as I write this: "When it comes to men, aim high! Don't allow just anyone access to your heart." A father's heart goes up and down the emotional roller coaster at the thought of his daughter trusting men who are clearly "frogs" and who will never be changed by even the most loving of kisses. The same is true for guys in search of a beauty to spend the rest of their lives with.

Every girl wants a knight in shining armor.

Every man wants a beautiful princess.

Women want to be pursued, to be loved and to be the heart's desire of a mysterious knight. But a knight's armor has a metal flap over the face area, and before she marries him, a woman needs to open the flap and see who is really inside there! That's all I'm saying.

Men want to win the heart of a beautiful girl. But a guy does not want to find out a few months after his marriage that his wife is shallow, spoiled and obsessed with getting her own way.

Women believe in a man's potential and are wired to see it. God gave women an innate ability to see the best in a man; they can often spot fledgling talents, gifts and abilities in a guy and feel a desire to draw them out. This dynamic, however, can set a woman up to be a mother to a man, not a wife, because she wants to help him grow into his potential.

A girl doesn't want to discover, after she commits herself to a man for life, that under his armor is a self-indulgent, self-focused, immature young boy—not the hero she was hoping for.

Don't compromise. You are amazing, and you deserve amazing. Don't let your emotions guide you in a relationship. Pay attention. Does he or she really love you, or does that person love the idea of having a spouse?

We have to be smart about love. Be love smart; be wise about the issues of the heart.

In matters of the heart, look for evidence. I'm convinced that men and women spend more time and energy evaluating someone to hire as an employee than they spend evaluating someone they date. A casting director takes more time selecting the right person for a TV show than many people take selecting the right person to cast in the real life drama entitled "The Person Who Deserves My Heart." Why does a woman who is intelligent and attractive, who possesses great character and ability, select a man who is not safe, is not going to treat her well and is not good spouse material?

Other men can tell that the guy she's pursuing is dangerous. Her female friends don't really trust the guy, although some encourage her to proceed.

Many women take the leap with certain men because "he has so much potential." Here's what ladies have to realize: every man has potential. Most people—really, *most* people—do *nothing* about their own potential. Put more value on a guy's results or progress than on potential alone.

From a Father's Heart

In addition to our biological daughter, Holly and I also have a handful of "adopted daughters" who have attended our church for some time. We love and care deeply about all of them, and it's heartbreaking to watch women we consider daughters go down the destructive path of risky choices that they can make with men. Why can't they use the same insight, skill and confidence they use in work or ministry and apply those to issues of their heart? Why is it that some women pursue "bad boys" or are attracted to men who are clearly risky and have "dangerous" written all over their lives?

When Holly and I were celebrating our 24th anniversary, I thought about people who, because they settle for a frog instead of waiting for a prince or trust a damsel in distress, may never get the opportunity to celebrate even their 10th anniversary. I sat down and wrote a letter to my daughter, who was 17 at the time. I wanted to give her some ideas that might help increase her chances at having a fulfilling marriage. Perhaps this can help you—male or female.

January 12, 2009

Dear Paris,

Today is your mother's and my 24th anniversary.

Those are kind of rare these days. Many times, relationships just don't make for a marriage that will last that long. Sometimes people stay married that long, but they just kind of endure it and don't really enjoy it like they once did.

My wish for you is that you enjoy a loving relationship and have a marriage that will last.

After having been married 24 years and helping hundreds of others in their relationships, I believe that a successful marriage has a lot to do with who you choose to give your heart to. A father wants the best in life for his daughter, and I'm no different.

You once said in a video message that when you got married, you wanted a man like me. You may not need someone like me (although I loved hearing that), but I do hope you end up choosing someone to give your heart to who will be a great match for you. As a dad, I would say to choose someone who is good enough for you, someone who is worthy of you. Ultimately, this is your choice—no one can make it for you. Others can only hope that you guard your heart above all else.

I've given similar advice to thousands of others, but I thought I'd share it with you on this special day in a more personal way. My advice to you, as your daddy, is to find someone who is:

1. A Christ-follower.
This should be the number-one thing.

I'm not talking about picking someone who says he is a Christian; we've met many people like that. I'm not talking about someone who knows a lot of Scripture or has been a church member; there are plenty of people who do those things who may not make a very good spouse.

I'm talking about a young man who has a genuine love for God.

Find someone whose faith inspires you to believe more and to live with a higher focus, a person who wants to honor Jesus Christ in how he lives and in the choices he makes.

This kind of faith will cause the person you choose to look for direction from a Source beyond his own thoughts and feelings. He will be compelled to be a servant at times when others focus on themselves; he will forgive when others want to hold on to little disagreements; and he will try to trust God when others just do things their own way. He will look to God's Word for guidance and will be accountable to God for his choices.

I've seen some people compromise on this number-one quality and regret it later because it affects so many other areas.

It has been so valuable to me to share a similar faith with your mom.

2. Respectful.
A person who respects you will think about your feelings and desires before taking action and making decisions. He will make decisions that demonstrate that he genuinely honors you.

Respect changes everything about how we talk to each other, how we work through differences and how we arrive at our ultimate decisions.

This kind of man will respect God's plan for your life. He will never encourage you or support you in disregarding what's best for your life.

Respect causes us to be kind in a way that others are not. It affects how we speak about each other to people and how we approach life together.

3. Protective.
This does not mean that he is *defensive*. He is *protective*.

To me, this means he is considerate of you. In our world today, it's easy to be self-focused. When the pressure is on, we tend to take care of our own needs first. A person who is protective will think of you before himself.

He will protect you physically from harm and from his own desires that would put you at risk. To young people this includes pregnancy and disease, but it also means that he will meet your physical needs in everyday life.

He will protect you emotionally by stepping up in times when you may need that extra sensitivity.

He will protect you spiritually by keeping a watchful eye over things that could be temptations and distractions.

He will protect your relationships, conducting his relationship with you in a way that does not jeopardize the other relationships that are important to you. He will not be competitive or unnecessarily jealous, forcing you to choose him in order to feel more important.

Love inspires someone to care for others enough to protect them.

4. A person with vision.
A person with vision has ambition with purpose. A person with vision has direction.

Some people may have goals, but vision takes a person somewhere.

Most young boys have big dreams. Some young men have interesting ideas about ways to make money. But ultimately, you will probably want a man that is focused on "making a life," not just "making a living," someone who wants to make a difference in the world.

Vision brings confidence, confidence brings strength, and strength brings greater vision. (Confidence is a quality that brings so much to a relationship, because it allows us to deal with situations that come up by focusing on those situations alone—not on our own hidden needs that subtly affect every conversation.)

Well, these are a few important qualities. Maybe you can tuck this note away somewhere and let it speak to your heart in the months and years ahead.

My wish for you is that you enjoy love in its highest form.

Love,
Dad

I'm not sure how much my 17-year-old valued the letter at the time, but I hope she keeps it and pulls it out from time to time to think about what I've said as she makes decisions about opening her heart.

Psychologist Dr. Gordon Livingston writes,

> The choices we make, choices on which our happiness largely depends, involve judgments about the people we encounter as we travel through life. Whom can we trust? Who will bring out the best in us? Who will betray us? Who will save us from ourselves? These judgments are important in direct proportion to the closeness of relationship. If we are deceived by a salesperson, we have lost only money. If we give our hearts to someone unworthy of the gift, we lose more than we can afford.[1]

The secret to finding love that will last is to clarify what you want and then to say no to every person who does not fit that picture. He's a frog. Learn to say no. When you can't say no, you end up in a relationship that is okay but not great, or great in some ways and mediocre in others—what I like to call a "better than nothing" relationship. But the BTN relationship really *isn't* better than nothing; it hacks away at your self-esteem and makes you question your judgment.

The best time to say no to someone is the first moment you realize that the person does not fit the picture that you and God drew together. This is easier to say than to do—it requires faith in God and in your own insight—but saying no can also be empowering. It is a way of declaring that you won't settle for less than you deserve.

Falling in Love—and Other Red Flags

She sees him. He smiles at her. She feels that special feeling down deep. Their eyes meet once more. The feeling is deeper with each look, smile and giggle.

Wow. Falling in love. What a great feeling.

My philosophy is this: *anything you can fall into—like a ditch, a trap or love—can really hurt you. Especially a ditch—and love.*

Our world is full of relationship tragedies in which we fall completely headlong and can't get up! Horrible choices, poor strategies, sad outcomes and desperate methods always produce dismal results. Without realizing it, women and men use the same pitiful approaches to love and relationships over and over again, yet somehow expect different results.

We have to be smarter about love. Be love smart. Be smarter about the issues of the heart. King Solomon told us, "Guard your heart above all else, for it determines the course of your life" (Prov. 4:23, *NLT*). Who or what we allow into our heart can shape the rest of our life.

When you are driving and you see a worker waving a red flag, you know it's a warning of something coming up ahead of you. Red flags are warning signs. Red flags mean "slow down or stop—danger ahead." Let's talk about some of the red flags of risky relationships.

Red Flag 1: Too Close, Too Soon

One big mistake people make is going too fast. Learn how to pace yourself; be careful not to get involved too quickly or to let your emotions go without restraint. Don't say too much too soon about the intimate desires of your heart. When you allow yourself to feel things too deeply and strongly before you know the person very well, you set yourself up for heartache. Don't allow a person access to your heart before you know that he or she can be trusted.

If you're the kind of person who tends to move too fast (or your friends tell you that you're the kind of person who moves too fast!), you are really not in the best position to be dating. Some people think that maturity is an age issue—"I'm old enough to date; I'm 16!"—but it's really not a matter of age. Maturity is more a matter of the condition of your heart.

The Scriptures tell us, "Enthusiasm without knowledge is no good; haste makes mistakes. People ruin their lives by their own foolishness and then are angry at the LORD" (Prov. 19:2-3, *NLT*).

Don't have so much zeal that you are hasty and miss the way of wisdom. Slow it down. Many people don't understand that a major point of dating is to evaluate the other person's character.

Is she a good problem-solver?

How does he handle conflicts?

Is the person respectful of others, even when he or she is going through stressful situations?

Does the individual overreact and attack those close to him or her?

Here is the fundamental question about a person's readiness for marriage (and yours for that matter): Is it possible for this person (or you) to love someone else as much as he or she loves himself or herself (or you love yourself)?

Try to answer these questions—finding the answers is one of the main reasons for dating. Some think only about the excitement, the passion and the emotion of dating, but those are less important than the quest for answers—and that takes time.

I once heard Neil Clark Warren, founder of eHarmony, give a talk in which he cited a study from Kansas State University. This study revealed something interesting: Couples who dated for more than two years before marriage scored consistently high on a marital satisfaction scale. The risk of marital failure diminishes significantly with longer dating periods.

Despite this undeniable evidence, many couples think, *But we're different. We love each other. We will beat the odds. We pray; we read the Bible. We have God on our side.* All of these elements are good, but time makes all of them more effective.

On top of taking too many emotional risks too soon, some people also get too familiar physically early on in their relationship. I'm not talking about having sex; I'm talking about the physical expression of intimacy in a social environment and what that says to one another and to others—whether we realize it or not.

A young lady once said to me, "I'm considering this guy as a boyfriend. We've dated a couple of times. I'd like you to meet him and let me know what you think before I move forward." So when we were all together in a social gathering, I looked across the room, and I saw them. The way they were interacting physically—touching, hugging and holding each other— I thought, *You don't look like you are "considering" anything! Physically you've already said, "I'm yours. I'm holding nothing of my heart back from you."*

Let's say that you see a married man talking to a young attractive woman (not his wife) who is standing 12 inches in front of him. She's touching a button on his shirt, looking down and giggling, then looking up at him through fluttering eyelashes.

Would that seem appropriate to you? No! You'd think, *What is going on here?*

This kind of physical communication is too familiar, and it indicates an emotional attachment that is improper for two people who aren't married.

Even if the man was not married and the two were dating, that level of physical affection and familiarity may not be appropriate. I believe that someone should earn access to physical affection over a period of time.

Dr. Joyce Brothers reports that before getting married the average American woman has kissed 79 men.[2] That is a lot of research! (I'm assuming the stats are similar for men, since that's who the girls are kissing in this report.) Are kisses really so insignificant that it's okay to hand them out to just anyone?

There are a few good reasons for taking things more slowly.

First, we can't get to really know a person over just a short period of time.

It's always a surprise when I find things out about people I've known for years. It's not that they were hiding something; that particular information has just never come up before.

"I served in the military, and I fought in Iraq for six months."

"Really? Wow, tell me about that."

"I had this odd job once in Europe."

"Huh. You lived in Europe?"

"I know how that guy feels, because I was arrested once when I was younger."

"What? I didn't know that—what happened?"

"My dad died of cancer when I was young."

"I've known you all this time, and I didn't know."

This is new information. It doesn't hinder our friendship; it's just new information.

But you don't want to get information on your honeymoon that could significantly impact your marriage.

"I was married twice before."

"I've had an STD."

"I spent time in prison."

"I've been through bankruptcy."

"I am a Red Sox fan."

"Hello?! This is good information to have had—yesterday!"

Married couples come in for counseling and say, "Everything was fine for a couple of years, and then all of a sudden he stopped doing *this*" or "she started doing *that*." When I hear this, I know that some kind of need has surfaced that was there all along. It's likely that if a bit more time had been allowed before walking down the aisle, that need might have been discovered and dealt with.

I've also heard so many explanations from couples seeking pre-marital counseling about why they don't need to wait any longer—they are the exception to the rule.

"I know that God's leading me."

"I've never felt this way before."

"We talk on the phone for hours. We know everything about each other."

And so on.

Getting to really know each other takes time. Is it worth risking your heart and a rest-of-your-life relationship to skip three to six months of evaluation?

The second good reason for taking a relationship slowly is that we need time to bond adequately for marriage—and throwing physical affection in the mix confuses our emotions.

Hopefully, there are some pretty high emotions mixed into your relationship. That is normal. But emotions can make it difficult for you to evaluate whether marriage is the right choice. Is it possible that you have missed something? Ruling out that possibility is the benefit of pre-marriage counseling and of taking time to get to know each other better.

This brings us to another common problem: Many people do not get out of a dead-end relationship early enough.

When we recognize that a dating relationship is not going to grow long-term, it is wrong to keep going just because we don't have the courage to admit it. We should have enough respect for the other person to back out gracefully so that it doesn't become unnecessarily hurtful.

Many times people break up six months or even a year into a relationship—but if they had been honest, they knew earlier that it wasn't going to work. They just didn't want to be alone or didn't want to hurt the other's feelings. But it's better to hurt someone's feelings after a few dates than after several months, when the emotions are deeper for both people. I can't remember the names of people who opted out with me after a date or two. I've never gone to therapy over their rejection. It's the relationships that ended after six months to a year that caused real heartbreak.

We are taught in the Scriptures that we should not defraud one another in this matter of relationships, romantic or otherwise (see 1 Thess. 4:6). It's dishonest to let something continue on when we know that it does not have a future. If you're afraid of how the other person will react, isn't that further confirmation that you shouldn't have a future together? If you can't be honest with the person or are afraid that he or she will blow up, you are not with the kind of person you want to engage in a life-long partnership with. Healthy partnership requires honest communication and the ability to grow and change with the seasons of life—together. And since time is something you can never get back, don't waste any more of yours or the other person's by being dishonest.

The third reason for taking a relationship slowly is that when you do, you protect yourself from getting attached too quickly.

Protect your heart. Proverbs 4:23 says to guard your heart *above all else.*

Is that how you live your life? Is that your priority? Or is guarding your heart further down the list than above all else, trying to find somebody?

Above all else, not wanting to be alone?

Above all else, getting somebody to give you a call?

Make guarding your heart your number-one priority.

Can a relationship work if you get married after dating for two months? Yes, it can. It's possible. But there is no reason to put yourself in this risky situation, especially when the odds are stacked against you. Forever is a very long time, so what's the rush?

I'm asking you to consider waiting at least one year (two is even better!) before you get married. Get to know each other. Go through different seasons; go through various circumstances; go through good times and bad times together, because you want to be sure this person is somebody you can trust.

You could be thinking, *Ain't nobody got time for that.*

It's better taking time now than it is using more time to heal from a painful relationship later.

Over time, you'll be able to distinguish the lure of *pseudo-intimacy* from the real thing. We all have a craving for human closeness. But that deep, satisfying connection can only be achieved over time with openness, honesty and shared experience. In a world of impersonal associations, it is easy to be deceived by experiences that have the look and feel of genuine intimacy but are in fact fake. Pseudo-intimacy is primarily about self-gratification, while true intimacy grows when we are other-focused. Understanding the difference is the best guard against involvement with someone who cannot or will not share the deepest parts of himself or herself.

Guard your heart.

Red Flag 2: Lack of Personal Growth

Dr. Gordon Livingston writes, "The romantic idea that we can fundamentally change another person with our love and support is a dream seldom realized. . . . The best guide we have to future behavior is past behavior."[3]

A commitment to personal growth is essential to relational success. I'm talking about personal *growth*—not personal survival, not personal enjoyment, not personal accomplishment. Personal growth.

Great people are dedicated to personal and spiritual growth. Personal growth happens when you recognize a lack in your life and decide to change it. You identify an area in which you'd like to grow, and you begin to learn—you read a book, you attend a seminar, you take a class.

People who develop their thinking are interesting people. Holly has told me that this is one of the qualities I had that attracted her to me. I've always been somebody who wants to grow in the way that I think, in the way that I feel, or in what I am learning. It's common knowledge that men do not read books on relationships.

I do.

Men don't read books on parenting.

I do. I want to know. I want to grow. I want to learn. I don't ever want to think, *This is all I know about being a husband and father, so I hope it's good enough.*

Two people who are dedicated to personal growth are essential to a healthy relationship. Everyone has problems, and we must all work on those problem areas of our life, whether they are spiritual or emotional. Then, as we grow as individuals, we become confident in who we are and don't need to force our perspective or will on others. We become flexible and adaptable, two qualities that smooth the rough patches that inevitably arise in the course of life.

Our celebrity-crazed culture is consumed with appearance. Billions of dollars are spent each year on diet pills, cosmetics, surgeries, personal trainers and the latest fad diets. We ought to put at least as much effort into developing our heart, soul and relationships as we put into our physical health and appearance. The payoff is even greater.

A physical trainer told me, "When you lift weights, you can't just do the same exercise all the time. You've got to confuse your muscles. You've got to change the exercise, or else your muscles kind of anticipate what you're going to do and find the easiest way to achieve it." This is easy for me. I just walk into a gym and lift one weight—and my muscles are plenty confused. The point is that it takes time and effort to have an effective workout strategy. One kind of workout may work for a while, but then we need to change things a little. A person who really wants to reach certain physical results will do what he or she needs to do. The same is true in the area of personal growth. A person who really wants to grow will continue to put effort into improving his or her attitude, motivation and character.

When you're in a relationship, you're the only one who can change. You are in charge of yourself. You can't afford to think, *If my spouse changes, then I'll change.* This is why it's so important to see clear evidence that the person to whom you trust your heart is someone who has a continual desire to grow. Growth will always be necessary in life, and growing will always be part of the solution to relationship issues. If your mate refuses to grow through the current circumstantial limitations, then the depth of your relationship can come to a halt. When your mate digs his or her heels into the ground on any subject, you are left to prayer and just loving that person as he or she is.

If you're single, pursue confidence and contentment at this stage in your life. Don't wait, thinking that some person will be the answer to your discontent and self-esteem issues: "I am unhappy now, but if I find someone and begin a relationship, I'll feel better and be better." The person to whom you join your heart should be an incredible addition to your life—that's the benefit of a relationship—but you must take the initiative to grow whether you are in a relationship or not.

Someone once said to me, "Philip, pray for me—I'm single."

Being single is not a sickness from which you need to be healed. You can be single, focused and fulfilled.

I hope you think, *I love my life. I like where I'm going. I'm content right now.* Be careful about the insidious belief that a partner will bring wholeness to you. Two incomplete lives can't make a whole; you must both seek healing, wholeness and growth in God. Then together you can accomplish amazing things.

A commitment to growing in heart and mind, whether you're single, dating or married, will allow you to live from greater strength, interacting with people and handling situations without being paralyzed by neediness.

Red Flag 3: Too Many Incompatibilities
A strong relationship needs a foundation of similarities and common connection. Holly and I often laugh about how different we are—the

standard differences between men and women, personality differences and differing levels of energy—but too many differences can bury a relationship. We have learned to find value in our differences. She brings strengths that I don't have to our marriage. I bring strengths that she doesn't have to our marriage.

Having said all that, we don't underestimate the power of our similarities in the most important areas of our relationship. Common values and interests allow couples to work through their differences, and it is what we have in common that makes us so compatible. C. E. Rollins, in his book *Are We Compatible?* writes that compatible couples have a strong foundation of similarities in background, temperament, goals, dreams and values, and have similar ways of managing their mental and physical lives.[4]

To be honest with you, Holly and I have what I would call "irreconcilable differences." I will never think the way she thinks. I'll never have the emotions and thoughts of a woman. She'll never think like a man. But we've learned to love and respect each other and our unique approaches to life. And those irreconcilable differences are not going to break up our relationship, because we also have some strong unified values. We share a strong sense of vision, and we agree about the priorities in our life. These priorities define us—family, ministry, fun and what contentment really means—and they allow us to navigate through our differences.

I believe that the number-one hindrance to a great marriage is dealing with differences. I think that the longer you're married, many times, the more different you are. It could be that the most similar you and your spouse will ever be is when you first get married.

Don't be careless and think that your differences don't matter very much. One day you'll hit the wall and wonder, *What are we going to do now? Maybe I married the wrong person.* You will need to know and trust that your core values are compatible, in spite of your differences.

Areas of compatibility that can be crucial are:

- Emotional compatibility
- Physical compatibility
- Compatible energy levels

- Cultural similarity
- Spiritual unity
- Recreational enjoyment

Emotional compatibility. This is about being in tune with each other in the areas of needs, expectations, goals and dreams. Being in sync with each other about what brings a sense of contentment in life is important. These are the things that bring joy and satisfaction in life. Without emotional compatibility, one person can be happy and the other discontent in the same set of circumstances.

Physical compatibility. It's important to be physically attracted to each other, yet some people are tempted to ignore this aspect and over-spiritualize their relationship. They believe that because they share the same faith, it will be enough to sustain them. Faith *is* important, but physical chemistry is also significant. Yes, appearances will change over the years—some parts will wrinkle and others will sag—but that fact doesn't diminish the value of a basic attraction between spouses.

Compatible energy levels. An older man who had been married to his wife for 50 years was sitting on the sofa. His wife yelled downstairs to him, "Honey, come upstairs and make love to me!" His first thought was, *I don't have the energy to do both.*

Holly and I have different temperaments. I have a more introverted personality and a lower energy level, and I'm eight years older than she is. When she wants to do more, I want to do less. When I want to go out, she wants to stay home. Sometimes when we go out to dinner, she has a glass of wine and I have a double latte in hopes that this will bring our energy to a similar level—we are hoping to meet somewhere in the middle. (It has never worked.)

In your relationship one spouse may want an active vacation, and the other may prefer a relaxing time of rejuvenation. The husband may see adventure as the ideal way to enjoy a night together, while the wife's desire is for a quiet evening, watching a movie at home. Energy and activities can be negotiated, but it's important to be aware of these differences.

Cultural similarity. Your "culture" is the combination of your background, family heritage and growing-up experiences. We have many interracial couples in our church. It's a beautiful thing; we love it. But as pastors, we also aren't shy about reminding partners that their cultural differences may have to be worked out as time goes on. Some people are excited at first about the "exoticness" of being with someone of another race. Their partner was raised in another country on the other side of the world, and it's exciting to be with someone so different—but that excitement doesn't change the fact that culture can be an influential component to harmony.

Even two people who are both white, brown or black can come from cultures different enough to create issues. Did your family open gifts on Christmas Eve or Christmas morning? Did your parents split up chores along gender lines? Does your family have expectations about how much time you will spend with them? Do you feel more at home in the city, in a suburb or in a rural area? All these questions have to do with your cultural background, and you and your partner may have to negotiate the areas in which you differ.

Spiritual unity. Mutual faith is important and should be non-negotiable. In fact, the Bible tells us that we should not be "yoked together" with unbelievers (2 Cor. 6:14). This is referring to our faith, our spiritual perspective in life. There has to be unity, similarity and connection.

If you are an unbeliever and you're dating somebody who is a Christian, that person must care about you a lot, as is clearly evident by him or her pursuing a relationship with you. But that person is, in a very real way, jeopardizing the depth of his or her faith by including you in their life. The reality is that if you continue together, someone is going to change. I hope the one with less faith will increase in faith, but in over 25 years of ministry, I've noticed that usually the person with more faith lowers his or her intensity and passion for God to accommodate the person with little or no faith.

If you are an unbeliever and you are attracted to or in a relationship with somebody who is a believer, I encourage you to consider that it is their faith that makes them so attractive to you. I challenge you to consider making a decision to become a follower of Christ yourself. The person who means so much to you may be another one of God's ways of reaching you.

Genuine faith guides our life, so as believers, we should be protective of our faith above all else. The Old Testament prophet

Amos asked the pointed question, "Can two walk together, except they be agreed?" (3:3, *KJV*). Too many people end up with a kind of faith that's politically correct yet empty: "I respect your faith—you respect mine." They don't want a Christian marriage; they want a peace treaty.

I've noticed an interesting version of faith in some dating relationships—I call it faker's faith. A faker goes through the faith motions in order to be close to the one who actually has faith. It's not necessarily sneaky, but it's not real. Men can change radically for a short period of time to impress a woman—some men even act for months and months as if they love shopping! Other men display an interest in God while dating, only to let their pursuit of faith return to an insignificant level after marriage.

A woman can act as if she loves some activity that she has never enjoyed before; she can even convince herself that she loves it. Then when the wedding-certificate ink is drying, so does her interest in that thing that is so important to the man.

There is a major difference between somebody who is willing to go to church and serve God just because it's important to his love interest and someone who actually has a faith that guides his life. (And, as a side note, this is another reason dating at least a year is a very good thing: it allows you to see the depth of a person's faith.)

Mother Teresa had a pretty simple mission. It was to love and comfort the sick and dying in Calcutta. Unfortunately, some people have unconsciously adopted a similar mission statement for dating and even for marriage. They pick a partner who is spiritually or emotionally sick and dying, who is unable to pursue a long-term, intimate relationship because he or she cannot give back. One person is the nurse, and the other is the patient—for the rest of their lives.

Don't make excuses for people. Love them. Respect their faith or their non-faith. But recognize that "evangelism dating" is dangerous to the heart.

Think about it: dating someone to evangelize that person is a relationship based on a hidden agenda. "I'm going to act as if I love you just as you are, but I secretly hope that you're going to have a faith like mine. I'll take you to church, and maybe you'll get saved, and then I'll fully love you."

Does that seem a little dishonest to you?

There's a hidden pressure coercing the other person. It's a spiritual audition. Do you want to build a relationship with somebody who has a secret agenda to change you?

Believers and non-believers aren't the only ones with differences; there can be spiritual incompatibilities even between Christians. Believers can differ when it comes to beliefs, doctrine, worship preferences and church type. Some believers put a major emphasis on missions in developing nations, while others are focused on local discipleship. Some like loud, energetic worship while others prefer a more reflective style.

If you disregard these kinds of differences and move forward in your relationship, you may find yourself in disharmony. Then, when you come to a point at which you're praying that God will intervene in your marriage, you realize that your faith is pulling you apart rather than bringing you together.

The powerful truth is that faith can totally transform a relationship, but your faith and your spouse's have to have enough similarities. Spiritual unity will help you deal with the difficulties that come your way in life.

Recreational Enjoyment. What do you like to do for fun? When you are dating, your parameters for what you consider acceptable entertainment will be much wider than they will be after you get married. Life gets hard, and for this reason recreation and relaxation become crucial to your personal and relational health.

You do not have to enjoy everything your spouse likes to do for recreation, but there must be a few things that both of you enjoy doing together. For example, I've always loved to ride horses. Holly and I have owned several different horses over the years. Holly has ridden with me many times in the past, but it just does not have the same impact for her that it does for me. So I ride with my kids or my friends or even get away out on the trails by myself.

Many couples whom we've counseled find themselves with a disconnect in this area—and the relationship quickly dries up. This is why I say that you must find some things that you both enjoy doing *together*. Find some activities that are fun, interesting, engaging and valuable to both of you. These could include hobbies, sports, exercise, entertainment or a particular skill. It could be reading, hiking, boating, ice skating, fishing, going to restaurants, playing cards or games—even playing ice hockey. It doesn't matter what it is, just as long as it builds companionship and recreation.

Red Flag 4: Emotional Recklessness

Emotions are great impostors. Emotions are convincing. They can make you believe that relational red flags are simply not significant in your situation. Emotions can make you feel as if you've heard the voice of God telling you to do something that the Bible would never support. An emotionally driven relationship is felt first and thought about later—and it's headed for a train wreck.

You have to have your "SART meter" in the on position. SART stands for "Something Ain't Right There." When the meter goes off, pay attention—until you are convinced that things are okay.

Emotions tell you to ignore your brain in matters of the heart. When they are in charge, a miracle takes place; it's called "brain relocation." Your brain ceases to function from the seat of reason and moves from your head to your "gut." (And when sex is involved, the brain migrates even further south. We don't make the wisest choices when sexually aroused, because sexual passion is easily mistaken for emotional passion—which is, in turn, mistaken for good sense.)

Isaac Hayes used to sing a song called "(If Loving You Is Wrong) I Don't Want to Be Right." That is the song of someone who is headed for disaster.

One of the most important abilities you can develop for relationships is the ability to turn your back on your emotions long enough to make the right decision.

Insecurities can be a destructive force in relationships. Insecurities will make genuine problems more complicated than they need to be. Cries for attention and poor judgment can be seen in a person if you are willing to take an honest look.

"I would go out with you, but I saw your Facebook page." You can learn a lot about a person by just looking at their Facebook page. Many people have missed out on jobs because employers looked at their Facebook pages and could see quickly enough that these people were not a good fit for the job.

People don't usually get pregnant outside of marriage because they've thought everything through; it's usually because of a poor decision made in the heat of a moment. It's an emotionally driven, sexually driven action that shapes the rest of their life.

Clear values and personal boundaries will help you navigate through emotionally intense situations. It's difficult to make a clear-headed decision about your sexual boundaries when your shirt is off and you're breathing hard. Deciding your boundaries in advance, when your emotions are not clouding your judgment, will help you live up to your values. (Keeping your shirt on while on a date is a great value to consider.)

People driven by their values rather than by their emotions tend to have more confidence in the face of the many circumstances life throws at them. They usually handle conflicts well, whereas emotionally driven people do not. Emotions crowd out peace and escalate problems.

An emotional person pressures others and tries to manipulate them. An emotional man may pressure his date to have sex and may try to make her feel guilty if she refuses—as if she owes him something. An emotional woman, on the other hand, may pressure her boyfriend or husband to give her everything she wants, regardless of his ethics or boundaries. Emotions can weigh down a relationship and steal the life from it.

We want to be in love and to experience the wonderful feelings of romance. We should be able to enjoy the feelings of loving relationships—but we can't be led by those feelings.

There are two important safeguards against an emotionally driven relationship. The first is to have mature, married friends who have the kind of marriage you want to whom you can go for advice. (The counsel we take from others is extremely important in shaping our relationships; it's a mistake to seek advice from single friends or from friends who are living an emotionally driven life themselves. It is smart, however, to glean wisdom from a counselor or a coach who can help you interpret your feelings and the circumstances you are facing.) Advice from mature, married friends helps you guard against emotional recklessness, because they have likely been tempted in ways similar to what you are facing. They can say, "I think you should slow it down; your emotions are taking over here," or, "Hey, this is a red flag. You're not thinking this through."

The second safeguard against emotional recklessness is to make a clear list of your values. You may choose to write these down or just think them through, but once your values are established, you do not deviate from them. They are written in your heart. You talk about and deeply believe these values, and they guide you and shape your life.

Red Flag 5: The Absence of Service

When it comes to clothing, Holly does not see wrinkles. I'm not sure why.

"Holly, are you going out like that?"

"Yes, why?"

"Your dress is wrinkled."

"It's not that bad. No one can see it," she says nonchalantly.

"Trust me on this one, they can see it. I'm a person, and I can see it," I throw in as evidence.

"It doesn't matter."

"Take it off; I'll iron it," I offer.

"You really think it needs ironing, or are you just trying to get my clothes off?"

I have become the official ironing person in our home. You can call me Iron Man.

The point is that I serve the marriage in this area and in other areas as well. Holly also serves in our marriage. We each have to be willing to serve each other.

Jesus said, "For even I, the Son of Man, came here not to be served but to serve others, and to give My life as a ransom for many" (see Matt. 20:28).

All of us start out in life being "me-focused." We live in our own "YOUniverse." But relationships require a servant's attitude in order to flourish. Jesus said, "Whoever wants to become great among you must be your servant" (Matt. 20:26).

When we read the apostle Paul's instructions about marriage in Ephesians 5, he begins his direction with, "Submit to one another out of reverence for Christ" (5:21). Only after stating this does he talk about the roles of the husband and the wife. Marriage requires a mutual yielding and an intention to serve the other person.

When we are single, we tend to live thinking that life is all about us. It's not. It's not all about what we feel, about expressing ourselves or about fulfilling our dreams. What's going to make a relationship flourish is not making your dreams come true as much as getting really good at serving each other.

When you are looking at a life-partner candidate, ask yourself this important question: Does he or she serve others in any capacity?

Does he help out with errands or household tasks when the need is there?

Does she visit sick friends or family without complaining?

Is the person willing to do family projects or chores without expecting a standing ovation?

Does he or she volunteer at church and not keep track of the hours?

Is he willing to be a mentor to disadvantaged youth?

Is she involved in causes in the local community that don't necessarily benefit her?

Is the person others-minded?

How about you? Do you serve others easily—or at all?

Do you expect your husband to do everything for you?

Do you expect your future wife to take care of everything you don't want to? I like the book on marriage entitled *Your Wife Is Not Your Momma*. It suggests a major wake-up call.

All of us have room to grow in this area. To evaluate a person you are dating, I suggest you develop your own private "servant scale." On a scale of one to ten, is the person a two or a six? Be honest. Pay attention. After some time has gone by, reevaluate; has his or her rating gone up or down? If the individual's "serve-itude" has increased, great! But if it holds steady at a two or a three, look deeply into the person's eyes and see if you don't glimpse red flags waving in the distance. If this person can't serve others, he or she won't serve you—and marriage always boils down to serving one another. When people cannot make that turn, the relationship breaks down.

As Bob Dylan once sang, "You're gonna have to serve somebody." It may be your spouse. It may be yourself. It may be your own appetites. It may be others. It may be the Lord. You get to choose, but you're gonna have to serve somebody.

Think It Through

Women

1. Fairy tales are odd! How do you think a lifetime of hearing fairy tales has affected your perspective on love?

2. Do you ignore the red flags of risky relationship? Do you trust God enough to get out of relationships that could damage your heart and destroy your future? Why or why not?

3. "Over time, you'll be able to distinguish the lure of *pseudo-intimacy* from the real thing." Have you started a relationship and realized later that the man you're dating was not who you thought he was? Was he willing to grow and change, or did the relationship have to end?

4. Similarities in a relationship are so important. What are some of your core beliefs and values that you want your husband to have as well?

5. Go back through the section on red flags. Which red flag do you find yourself often overlooking? How has your history and life experience taught you to accept less than you deserve?

Men

1. Aim higher! Don't allow just anyone to have access to your heart. Do you compromise when it comes to love? Why?

2. Have you ever gotten too close too soon? Read Proverbs 4:23. Why do you think King Solomon instructs us to guard our heart above all else?

3. Similarities in a relationship are so important. What are some of your core beliefs and values that you want your wife to have as well?

4. We all have to learn to serve one another. What or whom do you serve—your appetites, yourself, others, God? What about your wife or potential wife—whom or what do you see her serving?

3

I Wish I May,
I Wish I Might, Have a Great
Marriage by Midnight

Holly

Dreams do come true, if we only wish hard enough. You can
have anything in life if you will sacrifice everything else for it.

J. M. Barrie

Through skillful and godly Wisdom is a house
(a life, a home, a family) built, and by understanding it
is established [on a sound and good foundation].

Proverbs 24:3, *AMP*

I loved Philip. He loved me.

Then we said, "I do."

And like Cinderella, I thought that this was all it took: love
and a wedding ring.

Cinderella lied.

Thinking that marriage is as simple as love and a wedding ring
is about as naive as thinking that all you have to do to get great
abs is buy workout shoes! Sadly, great abs come only after lots of
crunches, Pilates, Cross-Fit and diet control.

Unlike many women, you men probably already knew that Cinderella had lied. Real love is not quite like the fairy tales. Even still, maybe you are just a bit surprised at how much work a marriage takes. Sometimes when life gets hard, you might be tempted to withdraw or just play rather than do the work that is needed.

Please don't give up.

Randy Travis sings a song that asks, "With so much riding on the choice at hand, the spirit of a boy or the wisdom of a man?"[1]

Make the journey from a boy to a man.

A boy is a child. He is entirely focused on getting his needs met. This is not bad; this is just what children do. But when a male is 20 years old and still pouts, throws tantrums or slams doors because he is not getting his way, it's not good—in fact, it's a little absurd. I have seen grown men display all these behaviors—and if their actions don't accomplish the desired results, then the guys play all day, abandoning responsibility and the work necessary for building relationships.

Being a man means realizing that the world does not revolve around you.

A boy is concerned with taking care of himself; a man not only takes care of himself but can also do it while taking care of others. A man is an entirely different person from a boy; he's not just a bigger boy. A man will do the work necessary to build a family.

Building relationships is a lot of work. Period. I don't know anyone who has been married for very long who will not attest to that fact. Marriage requires a high level of commitment, loyalty and growth from the individual as well as from the couple. Our character in our relationships determines the success of our relationships. So when couples do the right kind of work—character work—more happiness and a deeper level of intimacy than they thought possible are discovered. But these rewards always come as a result of hard work and after going through some difficult moments.

And what are some of those difficult moments? There are various seasons in a marriage. Conflicts, fears, old traumas, big and small rejections, arguments and hurt feelings—or the disillusionment of someone being different than we imagined he or she would be. All these things are normal, and all these things are workable. And if people work through them, they reach happiness again, usually a happiness of a deeper and better sort than they otherwise would. They just have to do the work.

A counselor relates this story:

I was talking to a young man one day about his girlfriend. He was thinking about getting married, and he had questions about their relationship. Several times during the conversation, he said that something she did or something about the relationship did not "make him happy." It was clear that this was a theme for him. She was not "making him happy."

When I asked, I found that she wanted him to deal with some things in the relationship. He needed to do some work that took effort. It was not a "happy" time. When he had to work on the relationship, he no longer liked it.

At first, I was trying to understand what the difficulties were, but the more I listened, the more I saw that *he* was the difficulty. His attitude was, "If I am not happy, something bad must be happening." And his immediate conclusion was always that the "bad" was in someone else, not him. From his perspective, he was not part of any problem, much less part of the solution. Finally I had heard about as much as I could take of his self-centered ramblings.

"I think I know what you should do."

"What?" he asked.

"Get a goldfish."

Looking at me as if I were a little crazy, he asked, "What are you talking about?"

"It sounds to me like that is about the highest level of relationship you are ready for. Forget the marriage thing."

"What do you mean by the highest level of relationship?"

"Well even a dog makes demands on you. . . . [A dog has to be] let out to go to the bathroom. You have to clean up after it. Other times, it requires time from you when you don't want to give it. A dog might interfere with your happiness. Better get a goldfish. A goldfish doesn't ask for much. But a woman is completely out of the question."[2]

Sort of funny—right?

Fairy Tales

Great marriages are not genetic. They don't happen just because we want one. If they did, everyone everywhere would have a great marriage.

Having the desire for a healthy marriage is really only the first step in a long list of steps. And sadly, many couples don't make it past the first few steps. Desire alone will not build a great marriage; in fact, desire internalized and unfulfilled will destroy a partnership. No, a great marriage is built by deliberate effort.

But it's good to remember that struggling marriages don't "just happen" either.

On July 29, 1981, one of the most highly publicized and glamorous weddings in history took place. Great Britain's Prince Charles married Lady Diana Spencer. I remember watching it in the middle of the night—sighing, dreaming, loving all the regalia—and hoping that my future husband wouldn't have ears like that!

An estimated 750 million people worldwide watched the event. There were 4,500 pots of fresh flowers lining the route to St. Paul's cathedral, where 2,700 people crowded the grand church. More than 75 technicians with 21 cameras worked to enable the world to watch the ceremony.[3]

For many of us, this was a modern fairy tale. A royal prince weds a lovely lady in a grand cathedral surrounded by adoring subjects. Rich, young and beautiful (well, *she* was beautiful!), they were the envy of millions. It seemed to be the perfect match. But if you've been around the block a few times, you know that things are not always what they seem.

And sadly, we know how that particular fairy tale ended. The couple grew apart, and the storybook marriage we all wanted to believe in eventually collapsed into adultery and divorce.

And a few years ago, a new set of royals, Kate and William, had their own wedding with millions of us watching. And while it was romantic and so beautiful, we all know that it takes more than a prince, a lady and a palace to make a happy marriage. For marriages to survive, they require regular maintenance.

Right now, if you are thinking, *This is too hard. I must have married the wrong person*, then you are not alone. We have all thought that at one time or another. But your spouse is probably *not* the wrong one; you just have some work to do. Good times are ahead!

Real Love

A new command I give you: Love one another. As I have loved you, so you must love one another (John 13:34).

This is how Jesus is asking us to love others. Including our spouse. We are to love the way He loves. Not how we might have experienced love in the past. Jesus sets the standard. And it has very little to do with how we feel. Love is not a feeling. Love is not a place we fall into. Love is what we do, oftentimes regardless of how we are feeling!

Jesus' love for us was intense and consuming. He laid his life down for us. And that is how He is asking us to love one another. And then Jesus really pushes it, because in the Gospel of Matthew He says that we are to love our enemies. So no matter what your spouse may seem like to you at the moment—friend or enemy—you are to love them with that "lay down your life" kind of love.

So what does that kind of love look like? The apostle Paul describes it this way: "Not looking to your own interests but each of you to the interests of the others" (Phil. 2:4).

I don't really want to look after the interests of others, because the truth is, I am interested in what interests me, not in what doesn't interest me. Because what doesn't interest me is not interesting to me, so it would be hard to show interest in what is not interesting to me. Did you follow that?!

But we are supposed to have the kind of love Jesus did, which says that we not only look to our own interests but to the interests of our spouse. So I think that we should proactively express interest in what interests our spouse rather than just tolerate the things he or she likes. (Remember, this is real love—grown-up love, not childish love!)

For me this became baseball.

If you spend 10 minutes with Philip, you will quickly learn that he is a serious fan of baseball, and in particular, of the New York Yankees.

Since this is a definite interest of his, for years I have given him Yankees trivia as birthday presents—caps, jackets, bobble heads, posters, etc. As a surprise one year for his birthday, I cashed in some frequent-flyer points and sent Philip and our son Jordan to New York to see a game. I am sure they had a blast.

But you know what he likes the best about my efforts? That I demonstrate interest.

I don't just pat my husband on the head and say, "You go enjoy yourself, honey." I know the game.

I know that last season was Mariano Rivera's last one. A few years ago, I screamed just as loud as Philip—actually louder—when Derek Jeter broke Lou Gehrig's record of all-time hits and again when A-Rod hit 600 homeruns. I know that last year (2013) was not our best season, and I am hopeful for next year!

I made a decision to share Philip's interest in the Yankees. I knew nothing about baseball before I met him, so this was a choice that I made.

Another thing that Philip is obviously interested in is ministry. So am I. It is easy to share that one with him.

He is also interested in other things—horses, in particular—and while I appreciate the animals and think it is great that he enjoys them and all the smells of a barn, I am only mildly interested.

It's not as if I have to be passionate about each one of my husband's interests—just some.

Real love is caring about the interests of your spouse. Do you even know what they are? What is the thing in your spouse's life that your expression of interest in would totally bless him or her?

This extends further than just external interests but also to the interests of the soul. What brings your husband or wife peace or comfort?

What makes him or her laugh?

All this might sound hard, but if you want to have a marriage that 30 years from now still has that spark, then figuring these things out is something that you have to do.

A marriage is not a roommate situation in which you simply split up the chores and then do your own thing. No, this is a covenant relationship in which we love as Jesus loves. In which we serve each other. In which we are each interested in what interests the other.

That is real love.

Preparing to Be a Learner

Many people think that massive, miracle-like events are needed to change their marriage. That is not the case. I believe that it takes small tweaks to move a relationship to higher peaks.

It can be the seemingly insignificant moments in life that determine both our relational success and our character. I know that you don't feel like moving the kids' art project, the mail or your purse from the kitchen counter—but you know that the clutter irritates him, so love says that you have to. I know that you don't really want to hear the whole story of her recent trip, but she feels loved when you listen—and without the remote control in your hand.

Patience, generosity, understanding, affection, quality time and care all come so easily in the initial phase of a relationship. She watches all the games with him on television. He goes to all the chick flicks. She thinks it's so cute when he can't find his car keys. He opens every door for her. She dotes on his every word, admiration beaming from her face—these are the ordinary expressions of love that make relationships extraordinary.

In the beginning it all comes so naturally that neither of us can imagine ever getting irritated, hiding our feelings or growing apart—but these things happen. And they don't happen suddenly, with one major incident, as we might think. They happen in the culmination of all the little things: junk on the counter, a pressure from the other to "get to the point" that shuts us down, continual arguing over the missing keys. And then there are unspoken hurts, frustrations, irritations, hidden agendas, false expectations, unexpressed dreams—telltale signs of an unlooked-after heart that is constantly tempted to wander.

There are a lot of reasons for divorce.

Communication breakdown.

Personality differences.

Sexual frustration or unfaithfulness.

Money problems.

Unresolved issues from the past.

But maybe at the core of all these is just a lack of preparation. Most of us spend more time planning for the wedding than we do for the marriage.

And let's be realistic: it can't just be our spouse that is the problem (though there are days when I am convinced that this is the case). Sometimes we might think that if we were just married to someone else, then our problems would be solved.

I don't think so.

I heard a celebrity interviewed several years ago, just after her second marriage. The interviewer asked, "How did you know that this was the right one?" The celebrity just smiled and said, "When you know, you just know—there is this feeling." The last time I checked, she was on her fourth marriage.

Maybe her method does not work.

One out of every two marriages ends in divorce. That is *50 percent.* Can you imagine going to a bungee jump and hearing the man operating it say, "Come on, it's great! Two out of four people come back alive. Two out of four crash at the bottom, but wow, the fall is awesome! It's exhilarating. The anticipation is amazing. It gets your heart going—and, hey, we can make it a special thing if you want to bungee jump together. We can order flowers, have your friends wear tuxedos and videotape the whole thing. Maybe you come back, and maybe you don't. But we'll have pictures for your whole family."

Who is going to do that? Not many people.

And yet we jump into marriage. We jump into relationships that have a significantly lower percentage for success, and we say, "I know what I'm doing! I'm following my *feelings*!"

Sixty percent of second marriages end in divorce.[4] Some estimates indicate that 80 percent of third marriages can end in divorce and up to 90 percent of fourth marriages end in divorce.

Maybe we have a few things to learn.

We all expect our physicians to go through years of school and residency in order to be good at what they do, yet most of us expect to have a strong marriage without ever learning how to do it. Wouldn't it be great if universities required all students to take Marriage 101? In the long run, that class would prove more useful than the calculus class we take.

But for those of us who missed Marriage 101, there is hope!

We all need to remain students in our marriage, continuing to learn and grow. Why is it that we expect to spend time and effort becoming better at our job or career, which may or may not last a decade, yet we neglect to acquire new skills and knowledge about our marriage? I am committed to being Philip's wife until one or both of us meet Jesus—that could be a *long* time (not as long as it was 30 years ago, but still quite a while!). Shouldn't I get better at it as I go? Being Philip's wife is a role I will have for lots of years, so I continue to learn.

Good for you for picking up this book. That means that you want to learn and continue to develop your marriage.

Sadly, most people don't.

I want to encourage you to keep at it. Philip and I have read hundreds of books about relationships. Books about how to talk to each other. Books about what his needs are and what my needs are. Books about why he is from Mars and is like a waffle and why I am from Venus and am like spaghetti. We have listened to countless hours of teaching on the subject of marriage and we have attended many seminars together—all because we are committed to being the best at this marriage thing that we can be.

I tell singles that the number-one question to ask themselves about a potential spouse is, *Is this person a learner?* Because if someone is a learner, that person will learn to be a great husband, wife, parent, employee, whatever.

I learned in biology class that the way to tell a living organism from a non-living object is by watching for any change. If there is no growth or change in the object after a time, the object is considered inanimate. Dead.

It is the same with you and me as individuals and as part of a marriage.

We must grow. As individuals and as part of a couple.

As individuals, we must be willing to learn new things and think new thoughts. By thinking old thoughts, we won't make it through life the way we are supposed to. We need to meet new people, read new books, take new challenges and set new goals.

Basically, we need to be lifelong students.

A few years ago I heard about a group of nuns whose members consistently lived to be more than 100 years of age. Wow! Some scientists went to the nuns' convent to study these sisters and find out what was different about how they lived. Certainly their lives were more organic and pure than many people's, but the scientists also discovered something else. They got permission to perform autopsies on the nuns who had died, and those exams revealed that the brains of the nuns had many more connections between various points than most people's brains. These connections are formed when the brain learns something new. The scientists then discovered, after interviewing some of the nuns, that the group was committed to learning new things, right up until death. They were reading new books and learning to speak new languages all the way into their 90s. Because their brains were continually growing and being used, the nuns lived longer.[5]

You and I need to be people who want to learn new things—not only so that our lives will be longer but also that they will be fuller. The growth that I make and the changes I embrace won't change who I am, but they will make me a better me.

Pienso que esto es una buena idea.

> Je pense que c'est une bonne idée.
> Ich denke, dass dieses eine gute Idee ist.
> Σκέφτομαι ότι αυτό είναι μια καλή ιδέα.
> Iay inkthay isthay isay ay oodgay idea-ay.

(I just thought I would help you with some of those brain connections!)

Most of us *say* that we want to learn new things. And we probably do.

But saying it is easier than actually learning. Once we realize how hard it is to do something new, it's very tempting to quit. But that's exactly what we can't do. We have to push through the learning curve.

My daughter is 22 and has spent years playing basketball. Thanks to her big brother, she has been dribbling a ball since she was a toddler. And after many seasons, she's a pretty good player. A few years ago I asked her to give volleyball a try, and she did. But after one season, she was ready to quit. She realized that she would have to work very hard to get good at this sport. It was new for her, and she wasn't willing to push through the learning curve.

Quitting volleyball is not such a big deal. Quitting on a marriage is. Quitting on trying to understand each other is.

We each have to push through the learning curve in our relationships. In life and in relationships, there are lots of learning curves.

As someone who is married, I've had to grow in a few ways. I've had to truly become a student of Philip—not only in learning his personality strengths and weaknesses but also in learning his likes, dislikes and needs. From knowing the simple to the more complex—his favorite food to what he needs when he is hurting—and then becoming willing for him to change his mind, which means I have to learn new stuff all over again!

The tricky thing for me early on was learning about him not to *change* him but to *know* him.

Some people come crying to a counselor, "He is not the person I married!" Well, probably not. And neither are you. Our tastes, interests and emotional needs change. That's what keeps things interesting, and it's why we have to continue being a student.

For years—23 years of our married life, to be exact—Philip did not like pasta. I think his mom fed him too much boxed macaroni and cheese as a child; when he thinks of pasta, he pictures packaged childhood meals. I thought this was a bit weird. How could a person not like pasta? Philip likes rice, and really, what's the big difference? Pasta and rice both taste like whatever sauce you put on them. For years I tried to convince my husband that not liking pasta was just wrong. I tried all sorts of recipes to entice him. Nothing worked. He did not like pasta.

My problem was that rather than being a good student of my spouse in order to know him, I was trying to change him. Not good.

But now something even weirder than not liking pasta has happened. A few years ago, Philip decided that he likes pasta. I have no idea what happened. All I know is that he began making reservations at Italian restaurants.

And just six months ago, he went back to not liking pasta! What?! As a woman committed to being a student of my spouse, I am just trying to keep up!

Philip needs time to process most things.

He likes the computer and television on when he is studying. He doesn't like human interruptions when he is studying.

He doesn't really like surprises.

He takes his time when making decisions.

He doesn't like interjections when he is talking. (He calls it interrupting.)

He loves learning things by watching a DVD.

He reads multiple books at the same time, not always finishing any of them.

The first thing he wants to do in the morning is turn on his computer.

He doesn't like long meals in fancy restaurants.

He enjoys walking at a leisurely pace.

And I am completely the opposite in every one of those—which can make marriage challenging! Because sometimes, deep in my heart, I wish Philip was more like me.

This is not good! It means that I have stopped studying who he is and instead am focused on who I want him to be.

I mentioned that Philip does not really like surprises. I found this out the hard way. (Well, honestly I knew he didn't like surprises; I just thought that he was wrong. Who needs to know every detail about what is coming?) One day, in the first few years of our marriage, I called his assistant at his office and let her know that I was coming to kidnap Philip for a few days, so she needed to cancel any appointments. I packed his overnight bag and made all the arrangements; we were just going to be gone overnight, so it was an easy thing to do. I got to the office and asked him to get in the car—and off we went! He was not nearly as excited as I was. In fact, he was a little bit irritated. He wanted to know where we were going and what we were going to do. And I was equally as irritated that I had to blow my surprise and give him all the details!

Looking back—and hindsight is indeed 20/20—my husband would have been much happier if I would have said, "Honey, how about if we go away for a night to Santa Barbara?"

Lesson learned.

Sometimes the differences in personality and preference can be annoying. But I have found that where I am weak, he is strong—and vice versa. We are attracted to each other because of our differences, and while they are often hard to work through, they make our relationship stronger. More on that in chapters to follow.

Ask Questions

Questions are a great way to learn about someone.

When Philip and I first started dating, he constantly asked me questions. Almost every time we were in the car, he asked me something.

It was great, because it meant that I was dating a man who wanted to get intimate with me by knowing my thoughts, my fears and my dreams. He was interested in the workings of my heart. How could I not fall in love with someone like that?

How about you? Are you asking questions?

Try these:

- What is your biggest fear?
- What do you want our life to look like in five years?
- If you had a million dollars, what would you do with it?
- What are two things you love about me?
- If money were no object, where would you like to go on vacation?
- What are you looking forward to?
- What makes you feel the most alive?

Over the years the questions might change—not to mention the answers!—but we should still ask them. The truth is, both of you are a mystery that will never be completely solved.

A stale marriage occurs when no one cares enough to ask questions. When we quit learning about each other.

Psychologist Dr. Robin Smith, in her book *Lies at the Altar*, suggests 276 questions that should be asked before marriage and then asked again during marriage. And they should be answered truthfully, not how you think your partner wants you to answer them. After all, it is truth that sets us free.

If you are dating and don't have the time to ask the questions, then you don't have the time to get married.

Here are a few of the questions she suggests:

- Are you working in your chosen profession?
- How many hours a week do you work?
- Do you prefer urban, suburban or rural settings?

- Do you think of your home as a cocoon, or is your door always open?
- If you had unlimited resources, how would you live?
- Do you have any debts?
- When was the first time you felt that you were in love with another person?
- Do you exercise regularly?
- What do you like or dislike about your appearance?
- Do you want children?
- Have you ever been alienated from your family?
- Do you have a best friend?
- Are you serving in church?
- What is your idea of a fun day?
- Do you enjoy traveling?
- Do you like to cook? To eat?
- Are there household responsibilities that you think are primarily male or female?
- Are you a morning person or a night person?[6]

Being a perpetual student is crucial. Not that you need to remain in college forever. Please don't. Learn and then do the work that is necessary. Continue to learn new things about life and about your spouse.

Wisdom for Life

Being a student and asking questions will produce knowledge. Knowledge is good. It is the first step toward gaining wisdom, and it takes wisdom to build a life, a home and a family (see Prov. 24:3). Wisdom is more than knowledge. It certainly requires knowledge about what is true, but wisdom is knowledge coupled with knowing what to do. Wisdom comes from experience—your own or, for the smart ones out there, that of others. You don't need to stick your hand in the fire to know that it is hot. It's enough to see the burn on the person who did.

Wisdom has a cost.

I have a lot of knowledge about cancer. I have read dozens of books and spoken to many health practitioners. I've also talked with people who have navigated their own journey and gained knowledge from them; in many cases, I learned what not to do.

But what I did with that knowledge became wisdom. I have gained plenty of wisdom navigating my own journey. I've learned that how I eat, exercise and rest really do matter. And wisely, I changed. I eat, rest and exercise differently. Knowledge became wisdom because I acted on it.

Interestingly enough, some of the people in my world now eat, rest and exercise differently as well. They did not go through a cancer battle; they were just smart enough to learn from someone who did.

Wisdom builds a life.

Wisdom also builds a home and a family.

We can get knowledge from anyone. I can learn from someone who has been married 10 times. Mostly what I learn is what not to do. But knowing what to avoid can produce as much wisdom as knowing what to do. Knowing what not to do is very good.

From a woman divorced two times: "We had very poor communication."

From a man divorced one time: "We got married too young."

From a woman divorced two times: "We didn't know how to handle conflict."

From a woman divorced one time: "He wanted someone younger." (After talking to this woman for a while, I realized that she was fairly bitter. She said that her husband had left her for someone who "thought he hung the moon." I guess he needed the encouragement that she wasn't willing to give. While her husband was certainly responsible for his choices, somewhere along the way his wife had forgotten how important encouragement was to him.)

I remember recommending premarital counseling to a man who was newly engaged. His response was, "Why do I need that? I've been married four times before." Why indeed? Guess he was not that interested in the wisdom that can build a home.

Because I am a student on a quest to gain knowledge, which can then become wisdom to build my own house, I have done some research on why couples divorce. The results were interesting to me.

Author Sharen Pittman wrote,

Divorce is one of the worst things a person can go through. It doesn't matter who is right, who is wrong, who is at fault, how much better one will be without the other or anything else. That may all be true, but in the quiet moments, it still hurts.

Divorce for many women is not only about the loss of a spouse and marriage, but the loss of a dream. You know that dream. The one where two people fall in love, grow old together and live happily ever after. It's the having just one person to grow old with, raise a family and build a life.

Divorce takes a huge toll emotionally. Again, cause doesn't matter. There are still feelings of failure and wishing things could have been done differently or not at all. Regrets and hurts take years to get over.[7]

It does not appear that only one factor contributes to a couple's decision to divorce; there are a number of reasons why marriages fail.[8] The number-one reason for marriage breakup given by divorced couples is a lack of communication or poor communication. The second-most cited reason is marital conflicts and arguments. Third, many divorced couples say infidelity led to their divorce.

While these are the primary reasons cited for failed marriages, statistics show that there are several underlying factors that contribute to these trends. Those who get married in their mid to late 20s are less likely to get divorced than those who marry at a younger age, and this age group also tends to be more satisfied in marriage than couples who marry later in life.

Education and income both play a role in divorce. Data shows that a married couple with a higher education and a higher income is less likely to divorce than a couple with lower education and lower income.

Reports suggest that between 40 and 85 percent of couples who lived together before getting married had their marriages end in divorce. Interesting, isn't it? Most people who live together think that it will help their marriage.

About 25 percent of adults in the United States have been divorced at least once in their lifetime. Characteristics of individuals who have a higher probability of divorce include:

- younger age at time of marriage
- lower education
- children from a previous relationship
- cohabitation prior to marriage
- sexual activity prior to marriage

As marriage therapist Dr. Jon Gottman notes:

One of the saddest reasons a marriage dies is that neither spouse recognizes its value until it is too late. Only after the papers have been signed, the furniture divided, and separate apartments rented do the exes realize how much they really gave up when they gave up on each other. Too often a good marriage is taken for granted rather than given the respect and nurturing it deserves and desperately needs.[9]

Now perhaps you are looking at those statistics and thinking that you are in trouble—because you were 22 years old when you got married, neither of you went to college, and the wife has a child from a previous relationship.

Relax.

Your marriage can be different, because you are getting the tools necessary to navigate the marriage adventure. If you are committed to being a student—to learning about yourself and becoming emotionally healthy, to learning about marriage, each other and life—you have a much greater chance of making it to old age with the spouse you now have! And not only to making it but also to loving each other the whole way!

Recently, I started talking to people who have been married longer than my 29 years. I am on the quest to gain knowledge. I have learned a few things:

From a man married 44 years: *Hold hands often.*
From a woman married 32 years: *Sometimes it is better to keep quiet.*
From a man married 31 years: *Let her do most of the talking!* ☺
From a man married 42 years: *Leave the house when she is hosting a wedding shower for a friend. Too much girl noise.*
From a man married 33 years: *Patience.*

From a woman married 30 years: *Persevere through hard times.*
From a woman married 35 years: *Decide that this is the man you want to grow old with, and do whatever it takes.*
From a woman married 36 years: *Smile often.*

All this knowledge will become wisdom if I actually *do* hold Philip's hand often—and occasionally be quiet—and persevere through tough moments—and smile a lot.

Sometimes it might seem as if marriage is too much work. Yes, it does require work, but the work is necessary to produce unity, peace and *fun*!

Before I began pastoring The Oasis with Philip, I was an actress in Los Angeles. I have worked on a number of films, and each one required a lot of work. A lot of time. A lot of hours (eye cream, coffee and inconvenience!). Yet the end result was not just days of work, but a movie.

The end result of your work—your learning and regular marriage maintenance—will be a great marriage!

So don't lose focus.

Perhaps we all have a little ADD. But don't get distracted from what you are trying to build. And when you do, refocus and get back to building a life with the one you love. "Let's not get tired of doing what is good. At just the right time we will reap a harvest of blessing if we don't give up" (Gal. 6:9, *NLT*).

Think It Through

Women

1. What is it with us women and the fairy tale? (Cinderella lied, remember?!) When did you realize that your fairy tale wasn't reality?
2. Are you waiting for a miraculous event to occur in order for your marriage to change? What small tweak can you make that will express love to your husband (even if it's cleaning all the stuff off the counter!)?
3. Think about the characteristics of your husband. Are yours the opposite of any of his? Is there a part of you that secretly hopes that he will change and be more like you?
4. When is the last time you studied your husband? Why not try asking him a couple of questions this week? What concerns are on your husband's mind? Is he working in his chosen profession? Take time to ask.

Men

1. Read Proverbs 24:3. How is a house (a life, a home, a family) built and established? What do you think it takes to build a great and lifelong marriage?
2. The statistics about marriage are not very encouraging; maybe we have a few things to learn. Are you a student in your marriage? Why or why not?
3. Questions help us remain a student; they are the natural verbiage within a relationship. When is the last time you asked your wife some questions? Why not try a couple this week? What is your wife afraid of? Is she investing her time in the things that are on her heart? She will love that you asked.
4. Wisdom builds a home, a life, a family—and wisdom has a cost. What price have you had to pay for your wisdom?

4

The E5 Solution

Philip

No woman ever woke up in the morning and thought,
"I sure hope no one sweeps me off my feet today."
Hitch, from the movie *Hitch*

Each one of you also must love his wife as he loves himself,
and the wife must respect her husband.
The apostle Paul, Ephesians 5:33

If you've ever traveled on an airline, you've heard some version of the preflight speech or video: "Buckle your seat belts," "The exits are behind you," etc. And my personal favorite: "In the unlikely event of a water landing . . ." Which, in my opinion, is another way of saying, "If we crash into the ocean . . ."

Did you ever notice that in the video, everyone on the video is calmly attending to the emergency instructions with a smile on their faces? I can't imagine that this would be real. Most of us have a look of panic on our faces during a crisis. I usually start to get uneasy just from waiting until the little light shaped like people and a toilet turns green.

The one that really gets me to think about a values conflict is, "If we experience a sudden loss of cabin pressure and you have small children, put your mask on first and then help the child."

While at first it seems as if this could be a selfish act, the reason for this instruction is because of something called hypoxia. When there is a reduction of air in the lungs, the brain loses oxygen, which results in sluggish thinking, dimmed vision and a loss of consciousness. You have to be able to think clearly first, or you won't be able to help anyone else.

Hypoxia can set in fast—before we realize it.

And then it's too late.

The strange thing is that a person affected by hypoxia is not conscious of it. Some people can start laughing, and others can get disoriented. They may not even realize that there is a danger and they can no longer control their functions, and they could pass out.

This makes me think about marriage and relationships, because passionate relationships require oxygen. And when life goes out of a relationship, often we are not conscious of it. We have sluggish thinking, dimmed vision and a loss of consciousness in our marriage, romantically speaking. Then the next thing we know, our relationship needs CPR or even mouth-to-mouth resuscitation. The second option, by the way, can be a lot of fun.

The Tumultuous Downward Spiral

Relationships and marriage can be either wonderful or devastating.

Or both.

There is something we can do about the direction our marriage takes. But it is up to us to be proactive about it. It turns out that we don't have to make a horrible mistake to mess up our marriage. *All we have to do is—nothing.*

I heard it said, "There is seldom something more beautiful than a calm sea at sunset—and few things more terrible than the storm at sea."

Once we've been married for a while, men and women can begin to take each other for granted. We get used to the awesomeness of the other and begin to try to tweak things just a bit. "If he could change in this area, we'd be amazing." We neglect the important things. We forget what brings love into a relationship.

Men can have a tendency to gravitate toward becoming inattentive, especially when the relationship has been going for a while.

We can become clueless. And suddenly we are simply unaware of what our wife needs.

We are unaware that she is hurting, unaware that she needs to be reassured or unaware that she may be drifting from the purpose of God in her life.

In the story of the Garden of Eden, we read that Satan was tempting Eve with the allure of "a better way to go." With the destiny of all humanity at stake, Adam was somewhere under a tree, watching the NBA finals, completely unaware of what was happening.

We don't see him stand up for Eve, protest the devil's suggestion—Adam did not step up to the plate.

Women, on the other hand, have a tendency to become "relationship experts." They may think they know all about relationships but be unaware of the changes in their own husband and in his needs, and they may disregard the idea that he could be growing and changing. Men don't want to be diagnosed—they want to be loved.

Many people today have a fear that love does not work! You can't blame them because of what we see around us.

The reality is this:

Manipulation does not work. Love works.

Criticism does not work. Love works.

Lust does not work. Love works.

Control does not work. Love works.

The truth is that love *does* work. We just forget how to love.

People get hurt through disappointments and then stop trusting each other. We stop trusting ourselves. We don't trust our ability to have good relationships.

In our society today many people don't believe that the idea of marriage is relevant. Couples live together as though they were married in order to practice or to test the waters. They do this rather than actually getting married, because they think that marriage is too risky.

Even though the statistics are clear—over 50 percent of couples who cohabitate before marriage are broken up within five years[1]—people still want to try things out first, thinking that this will better prepare them. But that's a false assumption.

It does not work.

Marriage without love does not work. Marriage with love works amazingly. But examples of a good marriage are rare. We see friends or family members who seem as if they should have a great marriage but whose relationship begins to fall apart just like everyone else's. It's discouraging. "If it can happen to them—it can happen to us," we say.

Holly and I live near the Hollywood area of Los Angeles. In our city 20 years of marriage is a rare achievement. And when you hear that someone has been married for 40 years, you might think that maybe they just took a deep breath and struggled through it.

We are asked so often, "You've been married for 29 years? Wow! How did you do it? What's the secret?"

If you will do what others will not do, you can have what others will never have.

I challenge you to make your marriage a masterpiece. I dare you to join the community of those who enjoy marriage and who passionately recommend it to others.

The E5 Solution

You have a 100 percent chance of having a great marriage. You can have a great experience in your dating experience and in the search of finding the person you want to marry. This is possible when you remember the secret I'm going to tell you.

I am about to show you an amazing secret that can radically change any marriage. I call this secret the E5 solution.

One of the most profound writings about the secrets to a passionate, life-giving marriage is found in Ephesians chapter 5—E5. Verse 23 reveals the secret—"husbands love your wife and wife respect your husband." Many people don't really like this recipe for a great marriage and don't want to follow its advice. Their conclusion is, "Marriage doesn't work."

Marriage *does* work. Marriage works when you discover the E5 secret. The E5 solution will help you understand how to love.

The key to a great relationship is *understanding*. That's it. That's all you need. Understanding. And patience. Understanding and patience, that's all you need. And passion. Understanding, patience and passion, that's all you need.

And a sense of humor. That's it—that's all you need to have a great relationship; understanding, patience, passion and a sense of humor.

And the desire to learn.

But there is not a more important ability to learn than how to love. The highest kind of love will always continue to grow. No one really "falls" in love—we do certain things intentionally in the development of a relationship. But these things are often missed by the other because of the romantic feelings that dominate our attention.

But if you will do what others will not do, you can have what others will never have.

Paul concludes his direction for marriage in Ephesians 5 by summing it up this way: "Each one of you [husbands] must also must love his wife as he loves himself, and the wife must respect her husband" (5:33). We all need love and we all need respect, but there is something about the priorities of love for a woman and respect for a man.

I picture the image of pedaling a bicycle to demonstrate the momentum that is possible in this dynamic. Pushing one pedal down brings the other one up. Push the other pedal down, and it brings the first one up. Keep that up, and you have momentum. In marriage the husband expresses and demonstrates love to his wife, which is him pedaling. His pedaling causes her to feel loved. As she feels loved, she pedals, and her pedaling is her communicating respect. Both of you pedaling keeps the relationship strong.

This is the E5 solution.

Husbands, love your wife. Love her in a way that makes her feel honored and cared for. Love her in a way that makes her feel safe. Protect her heart and her emotions. Protect her dreams. Treat her in a way that makes her feel that she is the most valuable person in your life.

Wives, respect your husband, because respect is the breath of life in his heart and soul. When your husband is respected, he will be drawn to you. Respect to a man is oxygen to his masculinity. When he feels respected, he will rise to any challenge, go the extra mile and care for you with greater passion.

Keep pedaling!

Holly and I have a high-maintenance marriage. Our marriage takes work to be awesome. We both have to pedal! If we neglect these E5 dynamics of our relationship, then we begin to expect more from each other than is reasonable. We begin to make the world revolve around our own needs. We focus on the flaws of the other.

We have to communicate clearly and with intention. We have to intentionally prefer each other. We have to focus on serving rather than being demanding. We have to focus mainly on our similarities and not our differences. But there are so many differences.

It is rare that one of us says, "This is what I think we should do," and the other replies, "Really? Wow, that's exactly what I was thinking."

It happens, but it's rare. It happens about as often as a solar eclipse.

Sometimes I say to myself, *Am I crazy, or is it her? It has to be her. I can't believe that she just said that!* Of course, *I* am the one who is talking to himself. *It has to be her.*

To the best of our ability, Holly and I determine to keep the main thing the main thing. Remember, if you do what others will not do, you can have what others will never have.

Honor

One of the biggest problems in marriages around the world is having unmet needs and feeling unappreciated. There is a tremendous stress in relationships when we get the feeling from the person we love, *I wish you were different than you are. I wish you would change.*

Behind every marriage problem is an honor problem. Either someone has stopped honoring the other person, or someone is not feeling honored—regardless of whether it seems that the problem is about sex, finances or communication. I'm suggesting that a lack of honor is the real problem. We are either not feeling honored, or we are not communicating honor to our spouse.

Basically, this E5 Scripture reveals to us that honor for a man is respect, and honor for a woman is love and admiration. We *all* need to be respected, and we *all* need to feel love, but how we feel that is unique to each of us.

The apostle Paul tells us that we are to show honor to one another—and he was just talking about friends: "Be devoted to one another in love. Honor one another above yourselves" (Rom. 12:10). This honor dynamic must be intensified in relation to our spouse.

Wives, honor his needs as a man. Husbands, honor her needs as a woman. (We will talk more about this in a later chapter.) Marriage works best when we are dedicated to the success of our spouse.

In one situation Jesus addressed some religious leaders and said, "These people honor me with their lips, but their hearts are far from me" (Matt. 15:8). In a relationship we can say the right things and do some of the right things but still not communicate honor from the heart.

Women need some romance. What is romance anyway? I like how Jimmy Evans describes it: "Romance is meeting an unspoken need of your wife in her language. Study your wife. She loves it when you study her. It says, 'You are on my heart.'"

The Adventurous Dance of Relationship

> My parents danced together, her head on his chest. Both had their eyes closed. They seemed so perfectly content. If you can find someone like that, someone who you can hold and close your eyes to the world with, then you're lucky. Even if it only lasts for a minute or a day. The image of them gently swaying to the music is how I picture love in my mind even after all these years. —Patrick Rothfuss

A great relationship is like a dance. We get a partner, find the rhythm, enjoy the experience and step on each other's toes as little as possible. Dancing is one part technique and one part chemistry. It is learning the basic moves, connecting with your partner and letting the music take you.

The TV show *Dancing with the Stars* has made ballroom dancing popular among a whole new generation of people. I haven't seen the show much myself, but I wanted to learn to dance with my wife. So a few years ago Holly and I took ballroom dancing classes.

I used to dance in high school and college at parties with my friends, but somewhere along the way, I lost my "dance." I was going to rediscover it.

Holly picked everything up quickly, but I looked as if I wasn't having any fun, because I was looking down and counting, "One, two, three, four. One, two, three, four."

I was trying to remember what was next. Apparently I looked as if I was trying to solve a higher-math problem or figuring out how to end world hunger while simultaneously moving my feet around.

The instructor said, "Philip, smile—this is fun. You are supposed to be enjoying it!"

"Okay," I said.

"One, two, three, four, *smile*. One, two, three, four, *smile*."

At one point the instructor said to us, "Let me give a couple pointers to both of you. Holly, you have to stop leading. Philip is supposed to lead."(Hmm, what an interesting relationship metaphor.)

Holly said to me, "If you don't lead, I'm going to."

"No, you can't do that," the instructor declared. "Philip, you are supposed to lead. Be confident. If you are uncertain, she is uncertain. Don't take such big steps, don't look down at your feet, stand up straight, be confident and feel it."

"Can I write this down?"

"You don't need to. You will just feel it," the instructor encouraged me.

"Can I have an Advil? Or a glass of wine? Or both? How about both? That sounds good."

We eventually got better.

At the relationship part. And the dance continues . . .

Learning to dance with your partner requires connecting with him or her. There are principles you can learn, but no two people are identical. You have to figure out what to do and when to do it. And how to do it. It is an art *and* a science.

How do you respond when he criticizes you?

How do you respond when she feels hurt?

Discover his love language. Uncover her likes and dislikes. Discover the most important desires in his heart. Uncover her fears, needs and dreams—and promise to give 100 percent to meeting them. Learn more about relationships and about marriage and then try to apply what you learn to your unique circumstance and with your unique spouse.

And don't forget to smile. You are supposed to be having fun.

Noah: You wanna dance with me?
Allie: Sure. Now?
Noah: Mmmhmm.
Allie: You're not supposed to dance in the street.
Noah: You *are* supposed to dance in the street.
Allie: Yeah, but we don't have any music.
Noah: Well, we'll make some. Bum, bum, bum, bum, bum, bum . . .
Allie: You're a terrible singer.
Noah: I know.
Allie: And I like this song.[2]

Dance when you are happy. Dance when you are struggling. Dance when you are hurting. Dance when you want to celebrate.

A great marriage takes a lot of work.

A lot of work.

But it's worth it. Really worth it. Because love works. Marriage works. In the midst of your labor, there comes a time when you will see what your relationship looks like from the dance floor.

We dance for laughter, we dance for tears, we dance for madness, we dance for fears, we dance for hopes, we dance for screams, we are the dancers, we create the dreams—Albert Einstein.

Marriage—from Disappointment to Romance

In the 1994 movie *Don Juan DeMarco*, a young man (Johnny Depp) is under the illusion that he is actually Don Juan. He gets a psychiatrist to help him get in touch with reality. The character he plays gets the dynamic results of the real Don Juan but is somehow disconnected from real life. He is in a psychiatric care center as he talks with his doctor.

The doctor who works with him (Marlon Brando) is a married man, and his own marriage has hit a dull, lifeless stage. While he tries to help his client, he begins to see what his marriage is lacking. Don Juan challenges his psychiatrist's marriage with these thoughts:

> *How do I love?* By seeing beyond what is visible to the eye. Now there are those, of course, who do not share my perceptions, it's true.
>
>   When I say that women are dazzling beauties, they object. The nose of this one is too large; the hips of another are too wide; perhaps the breasts of the third are too small.
>
>   But I see these women for how they truly are—glorious, radiant, spectacular and perfect—because I am not limited to my own eyesight. Women react to me the way that they do because they sense that I search out the beauty that dwells within until it overwhelms everything else.
>
>   And then they cannot avoid their desire to release that beauty and envelop me in it. So to answer your question, I see as clear as day that this great edifice in which we find ourselves is your villa. It is your home.
>
>   And as for you, you are a great lover like myself, even though you may have lost your way and your accent. Shall I continue?

I Want One of Those

Holly and I were recently with a couple who were really in love but not yet married. They looked into each other's eyes and giggled, and they stopped walking at random moments to hug and to smile adoringly at each other. Have you ever been in this situation?

Oy vey!

"How long are you two going to keep this up?"

And they continued, complimenting each other, touching each other's noses with their finger, playfully chatting with each other and fully engaged in what the other said. "Ah, that's so cute," they would say.

Holly told me later, "I want a boyfriend!"

Huh?

"I don't want to have an affair or anything," she clarified. "I just want to have a boyfriend. In case you are wondering, I mean you!"

"Oh, okay, right." This was a relief!

At first.

She said, "I don't need a roommate. I want a husband who loves me. If I had just wanted a roommate, I could have picked someone easier to live with."

Sometimes things sound good at first, and then *bam*, they hit you in the stomach. Point taken.

Good point. Fair enough, because I want a girlfriend. I want someone who admires me. Who thinks I'm amazing and can't wait to see me and hear what incredible things I have to say.

Love works, so we have to return to our first love. We need to do what we did in the first part of our relationship. We think that love just hit us one day and that we "fell in love." The truth is that we invested in that feeling of romantic love. It's time to reinvest.

Husbands, look for ways to communicate love to your wife. Ask her what makes her feel loved. It might be different than you think!

Wives, he needs your respect. Ask him what makes him feel respected. And if you are really brave, ask him what things you have done that have been disrespectful.

The dance continues . . .

I am my beloved's and my beloved is mine. —King Solomon

Think It Through

Women

1. Have you ever taken your husband for granted? Think about what makes your husband special and unique. What can you do today to show him that you notice and appreciate the person he is?

2. Are you a "relationship expert"? Make sure that in the process of learning about marriage, you don't miss out on your husband's personal needs. In what ways might your husband be changing and need your understanding and support?

3. Ephesians 5:33 tells us that a husband "also must love his wife as he loves himself, and the wife must respect her husband" (5:33). What makes your husband feel respected? Have you asked him?

4. When you encourage your husband and show him that you think highly of him, how does he respond? How does this action-response pattern build love and respect and a great marriage?

Men

1. Could your marriage be suffering from a case of hypoxia? Do you need a little oxygen to revive your romantic thinking and vision? What could you do this week to make your wife feel the way she did when you first won her heart?

2. What have you done over the course of your marriage to proactively work toward a great relationship? Or have you done—nothing? What are some specific things you could do to invest in your wife right now?

3. Are you attentive to your wife and her needs? Perhaps she is hurting, and you are unaware of it. How can you reassure her and encourage her in living out God's purpose for her life?

4. "If you will do what others will not do, you can have what others will never have." How does this statement challenge you? Do you want your marriage to be a masterpiece? Will you rise to the challenge?

5. What makes your wife feel loved? When you take the time to do some of the things that she loves, how does she respond? How does this action-response pattern build love and respect and a great marriage?

5

Irreconcilable Differences

Holly

United we stand. Divided we fall.
Aesop

What I do, you cannot do; but what you do, I cannot do.
The needs are great, and none of us, including me,
ever do great things. But we can all do small things, with great
love, and together we can do something wonderful.
Mother Teresa of Calcutta

At the beginning of creation God "made them male and female."
"For this reason a man will leave his father and mother and be
united to his wife, and the two will become one flesh." So they are
no longer two, but one flesh. Therefore what God has joined
together, let no one separate.
Mark 10:6-9

I am an X-Men fan. In the X-Men movies, there are a handful of people who have special, highly evolved DNA, which makes them different from everyone else. Each of these people has unique abilities. I must confess, there are moments when I wish I had some of their extraordinary abilities. How cool would it be to be able to fly? Or to be able to look like someone else?

The X-Men's differences make for an interesting movie, but in reality, as humans, we are more alike than we are different from each other.

Through the 1990s until 2003, geneticists conducted research called the Human Genome Project. This project set out to determine the complete structure of human genetic material. There were many intriguing findings, but the most interesting to me was the conclusion that human beings, at the genetic level, are almost 99 percent identical. We are way more alike than we are different.[1]

You might look different from me. Maybe your skin is darker. Maybe your eyes are brown. Maybe you have freckles, or your hair is curly. Maybe your feet are flat. Perhaps you are five feet tall, or your body responds differently to penicillin than mine does. All these differences may seem significant, but they make up only 1 percent of our DNA. All of us are almost 99 percent identical.

I think we might get further in life and in fulfilling God's plan if we focus on the things that are the same about us.

Sometimes we are so adamant that our 1 percent be recognized that instead of focusing on what we are all trying to do together—on what we can accomplish collectively—we let our 1 percent create division.

God put you and me on the planet at this time in history to fulfill His purpose—not our own. He made us how He made us so that together we would see His purpose done. We are all supposed to be working together in harmony and unity.

One definition of unity is "acting as a single entity." Unity is not *being* the same, but it is all of us, with all our differences, heading in the same direction—walking as one. French author Antoine de Saint-Exupery wrote, "Life has taught us that love does not consist in gazing at each other, but in looking outward together in the same direction." We cannot move forward together if we are obsessed with keeping track of all our differences.

Our unity is so central to the heart of God, so crucial to the planet, that Jesus prayed about it right before He went to the cross. In His prayer we find an invitation to oneness not only with God but also with each other:

> The goal is for all of them to become one heart and mind— just as you, Father, are in me and I in you, so they might be one heart and mind with us. Then the world might believe that you, in fact, sent me (John 17:21, *THE MESSAGE*).

Togetherness. Unity. Oneness. This idea is a *very* big deal to God—and has been from the beginning:

> And the Lord said, Behold, they are *one people* and they have all *one language*; and this is only the beginning of what they will do, and now *nothing they have imagined they can do will be impossible for them* (Gen. 11:6, *AMP*, emphasis added).

In the story surrounding this Scripture in Genesis, the people were using the power of unity to create something contrary to God and His plans. So God had to divide them. But the principal of the power of unity is the issue here.

I am still trying to wrap my head around this reality. If you and I become one people—not the same as each other, but a people united—and if we speak one language—not the same language, but a united language—then *nothing will be impossible for us*.

Nothing. Not the AIDS crisis. Not the plight of the orphan. Not cancer. Not crime. Not loneliness.

When we are united, everything is possible. We can feed the poor. We can rescue the hurting. We can reach lost people. We can grow thriving churches.

We can build strong marriages.

You and I must unite around the 99 percent rather than letting the 1 percent distract and divide us. Our differences are there to make life interesting, not to separate us from each other.

Yes, you are different from your spouse—but only 1 percent different on a genetic level, although it may seem like much more. These differences are supposed to bring strength to our union, but sadly they are often cause for division. We are different genders, have different personalities, have different likes and dislikes, probably come from different backgrounds; these differences can divide us unless we seek unity.

Cultivate Unity

Becoming one heart and mind with your spouse will take more than emotion, more than singing about it, more than writing poems about it. It will require more than lighting a unity candle during your wedding ceremony.

Did you light a unity candle as part of your ceremony?

It goes something like this: At a certain point in the wedding ceremony, two candles are lit, each candle representing the distinct lives of the bride and groom before their wedding day. The bride and groom each take one of these candles, and together they light the center candle to symbolize the union of their individual lives.

The minister might say something like, "As this new flame burns undivided, so shall your lives now be one. From now on, your thoughts will always be for each other rather than for your individual selves."

In most ceremonies the bride and groom then extinguish the two individual flames that symbolize their previous lives, because they are now forever united together in love.

I like this part of the wedding ceremony. But I know, after 29 years of marriage, that unity did not come because we lit a candle.

In reality, it is more like this: We each have a box of broken pieces and parts, representing our personalities, quirks and backgrounds. We have the chance to combine our boxes and to build something amazing. Maybe we should add a box of pieces to our wedding ceremonies to paint a more accurate picture, but here's the kicker: building unity takes a long time.

Establishing unity requires cultivation. The apostle Paul put it like this:

> I have a serious concern to bring up with you, my friends, using the authority of Jesus, our Master. I'll put it as urgently as I can: You *must* get along with each other. You must learn to be considerate of one another, *cultivating* a life in common (1 Cor. 1:10, *THE MESSAGE*, emphasis added).

Let's look at some definitions of the word "cultivate":

1. To bestow attention, care, and labor upon, with a view to valuable returns.
2. To direct special attention to; to devote time and thought to; *to foster; to cherish* (emphasis added).
3. To improve by labor, care, or study.[2]

Do I *cherish* unity? That part of the definition stands out to me. Do we cherish unity, or do we cherish our own way? Do we want to be right, or do we want to be married? Adopting a spirit of unity in our marriage means preferring our partner over ourselves, devoting special attention to him or her, providing thoughtful care for the other and fostering an environment in which our spouse and our relationship can flourish.

I am not talking about being a doormat or suffering through abuse. I am talking about the day-in, day-out laying down of our lives and our egos. Jesus says it best: "Greater love has no one than this: to lay down one's life for one's friends" (John 15:13). Although Jesus did physically lay down His life for us, and there could very well come a time when you and I might need to give up our life for someone, I actually think that this verse has broader implications. I think that Jesus is asking us to give up our way, our ego and what is convenient.

Do you know what?

Sometimes I think taking a bullet for Philip might be easier than laying down my wants. But cherishing unity means laboring together to build a life, a legacy, a living example of Christ's love for His church on the earth.

Cultivate unity.

"Cultivation" sounds like a gardening word. I am not a gardener, but when my children were young, I looked for projects to do with them. We had a large patch of dirt in our back yard, so I thought that planting carrots together would be a great idea. It was my kids' favorite vegetable, so I figured they would get into this project. I bought the seeds, and we went out to plant them. Each of us took our finger and made little rows in the dirt. We put the seeds in the ground, covered them up and watered the whole area. Eventually green leaves started to come through the dirt. Yay!

We were excited just thinking about the beautiful, big carrots growing hidden in the dirt. Finally, when the green leaves grew long enough, we went out to pull out the carrots. We took a big basket, because we just knew that we'd fill the whole thing up. Well, we pulled out carrots all right—but they were severely stunted. They were about an inch long and two inches wide. We were shocked! What had happened to our carrots?!

Because I had not cultivated the ground, the carrots had not been able to grow. The dirt was too hard. Bummer. (So much for carrots in the salad that night!)

Cultivation requires work, and it requires tools—tools like wisdom and patience. And a willingness to get a little dirty. There is no cultivation of anything without a willingness to get a little messy. My carrots did not grow, because I didn't have the right tools and because I was not willing to get dirty, to get in the dirt and till the ground. My carrot project was doomed from the beginning!

The ultimate purpose of cultivating soil is to produce fruit, not just to play in the dirt. The focus is on the fruit. Can we focus on the fruit that our unity might produce instead of on the hard work that cultivating demands?

Vive la Différence!

Recently I read a science-fiction book about clones. Very cool. This young girl had been cloned and so grew up with three other girls just like her. They all had the same name, same personality, same movements and lived the same life. There were no differences to create conflict. Together, they pulled off the perfect crime: While one was committing the offense, another created the perfect alibi by putting herself where witnesses could see her at the gym. (This story has absolutely nothing to do with this book, but it was thrilling, and I thought you might enjoy it. Now back to the point . . .)

Because you and your spouse are not two clones, you have differences—and those differences will create conflict. When handled with maturity, conflict can be a good thing. Conflict can deepen a relationship and sharpen us as individuals, making us stronger as a couple.

A couple's ability to deal with differences is a sign of their maturity. Children demand that others agree with them. Immature couples do the same. An immature husband calls his wife selfish and has a tantrum when his wife does not see things his way. An immature wife gets discouraged when things aren't perfect and withdraws in resignation, mumbling that "we'll just never see eye to eye." Such spouses cannot live with the tension that the other person may never change his or her mind on certain things, and they easily become prey to intruders who will agree with them. He might begin to think, *That woman at my work is so much more like me.* She might begin to wonder, *Do I have more in common with that man I meet at school functions?*

In reality, annoying differences pop up in any relationship. Maturity involves working through the differences in the marriage you now have. Grown-ups attempt to understand the other's viewpoint while holding on to their own reality. They empathetically appreciate the opinions of the other person and work toward a negotiated agreement based on love, sacrifice, values and principles. Differences do not create intruder problems; immaturity does.[3]

Philip and I have been married for 29 years, and most of those years have been great. But there have been moments when I wondered if we would make it another year. Our differences have been our biggest challenge. Honestly, we still face them—because Philip is still who he is, and I am still who I am. We have certainly grown over the years, but we will never be each other. I will only ever be a better version of me. I will never be him.

I have talked to hundreds of couples over the years, and every single one of them, at some point in their relationship, has said, "We are just too different. We have irreconcilable differences."

Well, duh! We all have differences.

Honestly, you wouldn't be attracted to someone who isn't different from you. (I think God watches us as we are dating and thinks, *This is going to be fun!*)

Marriage is a lifelong process of learning to love each other's differences. When I ask couples who have been married fewer than 15 years what they would change about their spouses, they usually have a list. But when I ask couples who have been married more than 40 years the same question, they usually say they wouldn't change a thing. What happens during those 25 years or so?

Couples who take on the challenge of understanding their differences grow to love those differences.

When we are dating, we might notice each other's differences, but we don't see that they could ever be a challenge, because we are "in love"—that brain-dead state in which reality is nowhere within reach. This is the time in a relationship when women will go to every sporting event known to man just because we want to be with him. This is the time when our guys will take us to chick flicks and say things like, "I could hold you forever." He can do no wrong. It all feels great, this cloudy, in-love, euphoric feeling. Awesome.

Experts say it can last up to two years.

Mature love is what we do when the exciting, euphoric feelings aren't there. If we want to cultivate unity, we must move into mature love, which is much stronger than emotion, because it doesn't rely on a cloudy feeling. If we don't move into maturity, then when the euphoric feeling is not there, we leave or withdraw, maybe divorce, hoping to find that feeling again.

I knew a woman who was in the middle of a divorce from husband number one. She had been married to him for about a year, and they had dated about a year before that. The exciting, heart-fluttering feelings just weren't there anymore—and she wanted out. She wanted those feelings. She wasn't willing to go to a seminar, read a book, talk to a counselor or get help building real love. When I met her, she had already moved on to the next relationship. She had found a new man, and all the exciting feelings were there. The sad thing is that she thought her new relationship would end up differently than the first one had. It didn't. After a year or so, she didn't have those feelings anymore. This cycle could go on forever until this woman is willing to take the journey of real love.

Part of that journey is learning to accept each other's differences and letting them bring strength to the relationship. You married each other because you wanted to build a life together. Hopefully, you are reading this because you still do!

So what are some of the differences we must learn to deal with? Differences of gender. Obvious. *Vive la différence!*

There are some great books out there, written by some very smart people, that can help you cultivate an appreciation for these differences. I will touch on only a few common gender differences here, but we should recognize that there are always exceptions. Your husband may not be the typical male, and you may not be the typical female—but there will still be differences between you.

In biology class, I learned that there are two sides to our brain. You probably learned this too. There is the left side, and there is the right side (complicated, isn't it?). The two sides are connected by a thick bundle of nerves called the corpus callosum. This bundle of nerves is wider in women's brains, which allows more "crosstalk" between the two sides of the brain.[4]

This difference in brain structure means that there are differences between women and men on a very basic level. Some are interesting. Some might drive us nuts. ☺

Women listen equally with both ears. Men tend to turn their right one toward the person who is speaking. This fact will not save your marriage; I just found it interesting.

Females are generally better at reading people's emotions, whether live or even in photographs.

Men seem to be able to rotate three-dimensional objects in their head, which is why most of them are generally better than women at reading maps. Women usually turn the map in the direction they're going. (Perhaps all the crosstalk between the left and right sides of our brains keeps our brains from doing its job—which is focusing on the map!)

So he can read a map—but can he find his socks?

Women are about 70 percent better than men at remembering the locations of items found on a desktop, which is why we can usually recall the location of apparently unconnected items.[5] (This is why we can find the socks that he left by the desk.)

When my children need help finding something, they come to me, because "we need a mom kind of search." Philip opens the refrigerator and yells, "Where's the mustard?" From the other side of the house I yell back, "It's on the top shelf!" I learned to quit being bugged by his mustard-blindness, because it is just the brain thing.

Women tend to talk more than men. This is probably not a surprise. (Comedian Jimmy Durante was once heard to remark, "My wife has a slight impediment in her speech. Every now and then she stops to breathe.")

Generally men talk to communicate information.

Women talk for lots of reasons—information is just one. We also talk to figure out what we really want to say. This used to drive Philip nuts. I would be talking away in my closet while getting dressed, and he would call from the bedroom, "Am I supposed to be hearing this? Because I can't."

I'd yell back, "Nope. I'm just thinking out loud."

We also talk to create a sense of intimacy. Men usually want the end result of the intimacy, so this is where they have to become great listeners. Not just try to listen as they watch the game or scroll through Twitter, but really listen. And women, we can help our men. I have learned that if I say to Philip, "Could I talk to you for about 15 minutes?" then he knows that there is a beginning and, thank God, there will be an end. Sometimes women feel the need to share every detail of our day, and really, men just want the highlights. That's okay. If you need to share every detail of your trip to the dentist, call a girlfriend. She will appreciate them.

Men and women usually handle stress differently. We all feel stress—and not all stress is bad—but we probably handle it in varying ways. Men generally isolate themselves when they feel stressed. John Gray, in his book *Men Are from Mars; Women Are from Venus,* wrote that a man goes to his "cave," someplace where he can shut off his brain. He doesn't want to talk. He doesn't really want to think. He just wants a remote control and a TV, or a ball and a court, or tennis shoes and a trail. I made the mistake in the early days of our marriage of thinking Philip was like me. When women are stressed, we want to congregate. We want to talk about it. *All* about it. We want to explore all the aspects of how stressed we are. I think I drove Philip crazy the first year, because when he was stressed, he would try to isolate himself, and I would chase after him asking him questions, which is what I would have wanted him to do for me. And he just kept looking for his cave. He would eventually want to talk about what was stressing him, but the talking happened after he'd had his own processing time. Very different from me.

Women are usually more intuitive about the needs of others. If I see someone shivering, I think, *I'll turn on the heater.* But usually a man won't turn on the heater unless he is asked. He figures that if someone needs help, they will ask for it. I used to get so frustrated when Philip couldn't tell that I needed a hug. My sad little face wasn't enough of a clue! But I learned that if I needed a hug or some time with him, I needed to ask—and he is happy to give it, because he loves me, wants to do the right thing and wants a "win." Men are not mind readers. They will not pick up on the clues, no matter how obvious. Just ask.

But while I have read many articles and books and listened to many teachings on gender differences, one thing I have discovered is that, in many ways, Philip is not the typical male.

He will stop for directions. More than once. I am the one who would rather figure it out without asking.

He can't fix anything. And he doesn't want to try.

He has no idea what to do with a barbecue pit.

He does not make quick decisions.

So while there are some typically common gender differences, you and your husband might not fit the box.

Isn't marriage exciting?

Background Colors

Philip and I come from very different family backgrounds. You and your spouse might too. A lot of the initial conflict in a marriage is a result of trying to bring our different backgrounds together. Maybe your mother was a stay-at-home mom who cooked dinner every night, but you are married to a woman who works and who wants to. The dinner hour might have to work differently than you're used to. Maybe your dad was controlling or abusive, or he isolated himself from the rest of your family. That will affect your expectations as you try to build your marriage. We can't pretend that our assumptions are not colored by our backgrounds or that we don't bring any baggage from our childhoods into our marriage.

Maybe you were raised in a home in which there was not much physical affection. I am sorry about that, because physical affection is a good thing. I was raised in a home in which I was hugged and kissed every day. I was told regularly that I was loved, and I was supported in all my endeavors. I saw affection between my parents—lots of hugging and kissing went on! Philip, on the other hand, was raised in a home without much affection. His parents divorced when he was an adolescent, and before the divorce there was a lot of anger and fighting.

When Philip and I were engaged, my parents came to California to visit me. Philip and I went to the airport to pick them up—this was back in the day when we could go to the gate to meet people!

I saw my parents walking down the jetway, and as soon as my dad was through, I ran, jumped in his arms and hugged him. He began to twirl me around. As I was being hugged and twirled, I caught a glimpse of Philip's face: his mouth was open, and his chin had hit his chest. He was stunned at this display of affection between a father and daughter.

As Philip and I began to build our marriage, we had to figure out how to navigate our different backgrounds. He liked the affection thing and wanted to have it in our family, so now he does a lot of hugging and kissing! But I had to be patient while he got comfortable with it.

Yes, Philip and I had quite a few background differences. He was raised in the United States; I was raised all over the world. He had four siblings; I had one.

Maybe you were raised with money, while your spouse was raised cutting coupons. You will have to have some necessary conversations to navigate how you want to build your family.

Maybe you were raised in another country speaking a different language, while your spouse was raised on good ol' American apple pie. One of the women in my world was raised in a mud hut in Kenya. She came to the U.S. and received her education here, and she ultimately married an American man who had gone to an Ivy League university. In order to marry her, I think the man had to pay a bride price of 13 camels or something to her father.

They have had a few background differences to work through!

The Language(s) of Love

Another difference we might need to navigate is how we feel loved. Gary Chapman's bestselling book *The 5 Love Languages* is a great help in this area.[6] In a nutshell, he says that while we all want and need to feel loved, how we receive love may be different from our spouse. We each have a language of love.

Because I plan on being married to Philip for lots of years, I want to be great at speaking his love language. Learning that language is my responsibility. If I speak the language I want to instead of the language that he understands, we will not have much effective communication.

Si yo empecé a escribir en Español, solamente las personas que hablan Español me pueden entender. Si yo sigue escribiendo en Español, las personas que no entienden Español se van a poner frustrado, porque quieren entender, pero no se pueden.

❧ ↗ ❧ ♌♍♎ ♈■ ◆□ ◆□♈◆♍ ♈■ ♒♈■♎ ♄
♎♈■♎◆ □■●♉ ◆♏□◆ ♍ □♍□□●♍ ◆♏□ ◆■♄
♎♍□◆◆♈■♎ ♄♈■♎♎♈■♎◆ ♏♈■ □♍♈♎ ♈◆❧ ❧↗
❧ ♏□■◆♈■◆♍♎ ◆□ ◆□♈◆♍ ♈■ ♄♈■♎♎♈■♎◆ ❧♄
◆♏□◆♍ □♍□□●♍ ◆♏□ ♏♈■□◆ ◆■♎♍□◆◆♈■♎ ♄♈■♎♒
♎♈■♎◆ ◆♈●● ♒♍♎◆ ↗□◆◆◆□♈◆♍ ♎♉ ♌♍♄
♏♈◆◆♍ ◆♒♈◆●♍ ◆♏♍♉ ◆♈■◆ ◆□ ◆■♎♍□◆◆♈■♎♉ ◆♒♍♉ ♏♈♄
■□◆♂

If I kept writing the rest of this chapter in Spanish or in Wingdings, most of you wouldn't read it—not because you don't like me, but because you don't speak Spanish or Wingdings. Only people who understand Spanish or Wingdings could understand what I am writing. Everyone else would want to understand—but just couldn't.

Gary Chapman describes five love languages. While we all like each of these expressions of love that he illustrates, only one of them is our "native" language.

The first one is *words of affirmation*. Verbal compliments. Words of appreciation. Encouraging words. Kind words. This is Philip's primary love language, so I better get great at speaking words of affirmation.

"You look great today."

"That was an awesome message you gave on Sunday."

Honestly, when I am irritated, nice words are the first thing to go. I want to say words to Philip—only they are not nice.

Another love language is *quality time*. We feel loved when we get time with our spouse. Uninterrupted, focused time. Alone time. Time when we are listened to. I have a friend whose primary love language is quality time, but it is not her husband's. He is certainly happy to see her, but he doesn't need lots of time with her to feel loved. He asked me how he could get better at speaking her language.

What we realized was that if she gets one hour a day with him, she feels totally loved. So that's what he gives her.

Maybe your primary love language is *gifts*. Now we all like presents, but you may feel loved when your husband brings you flowers or writes you a note or gives you something in a blue Tiffany's box!

For some, their primary love language might be what Gary Chapman calls *acts of service*. This person feels loved when someone does something for her: laundry, dishes, scraping bugs off the windshield, cleaning up dog poop, whatever. And a person like this might feel unloved if he comes home to find the counters are filthy, dishes are piled up and his car is returned with the gas gauge on empty.

The last love language is *physical touch*. This is my primary love language, so Philip has had to get great at it. Remember, he did not come from a family that spoke this language, so he had to learn it. It *is* possible to learn a language you did not grow up speaking. And Philip has. Obviously, sexual intercourse is part of physical touch, but physical touch is more than that. Holding hands. Patting. Putting your arm around your spouse. Kissing. Hugging.

We must learn to speak the language of our spouse's heart. The movie *Love Actually* follows a few different people on their quests for love. There are some fairly explicit scenes, so I can't really recommend the movie, but I do want to highlight one particular couple. The woman could speak only Portuguese, and the man could speak only English. He was a writer, and she had been hired to clean his house. Because they couldn't understand each other's words, they had to learn to communicate by other means. By the end of the movie, they had fallen in love with each other—and both of them took classes so that they could speak the other's language.

Speaking each other's language demonstrates that you honor and value the other person. Love is about giving, so you and I need to be great at giving. What does your spouse need? It is not all about what *you* need. But at the same time, I have also found that as I start giving, I usually get everything I need.

Sometimes we stop giving or trying because we are irritated. We withdraw. We hold back. Not good. Grown-up love involves going beyond. Learn to speak your spouse's language.

Good Personalities

Early in our marriage, personality differences were the biggest challenge for Philip and me.

Organizations all over the country administer personality profiles to their employees so that they can place people in jobs in which they will flourish and so that the employees will function better together. There have been many different profiles developed in recent years, but Hippocrates (460–370 B.C.) was the first to begin the discussion. It continues today with the DiSC personality assessment, the Keirsey Temperament Sorter, the Myers-Briggs Type Indicator and many others. I find these helpful—not for the purpose of putting someone in a box but in order to better communicate and understand the people in my world.

Each of us is usually a blend of a few temperaments. There is no right or wrong personality. No personality is better than another, and each has strengths and weaknesses.

Our personality is God-given. God created us to fulfill a purpose on the earth, and it will require our personality. It's interesting to me that two people who marry each other usually have very different personality styles. We are usually attracted to someone who is different than we are. This can be a good thing! We have strengths in the areas in which they have weaknesses, and vice versa.

Sounds good, doesn't it?

My weaknesses are compensated by his strengths, so that together we are stronger than we are alone.

Yep, definitely sounds good.

Only my husband's weaknesses can be very annoying. I am sure mine never are.

As far as personality goes, I am not sure Philip and I could be any more different.

I am the fast-talking, energetic, out-of-the-box, never-a-dull-moment kind of girl. I laugh a lot, see the glass half-full, look for opportunities to have fun and like being with people. I am goal-driven and make decisions quickly. I like people to like me, and am always a bit surprised when someone doesn't. I am a loyal friend. I make new friends easily and have kept some for more than 25 years.

That's the good stuff.

On the flip side, I get impatient if someone isn't moving fast enough. I often need the approval of others too much. I might finish your sentences for you. I can talk too much. I can be loud and just a bit pushy.

Annoying, aren't I?

Philip is generally mild-mannered. He is compassionate. He likes organization. He gets where he is going on time. He is very funny. He is creative. He is loyal. He is a great thinker and a perpetual learner. He is great at ironing (wrinkles upset his need for order). He notices details. He is a great planner. He thinks before he speaks. He listens.

There is probably lots more good stuff.

On the flip side, he often notices what is wrong before he notices what is right. He can be critical. He likes things to go a certain way, and when they don't, it affects him. He can be slow to make decisions.

And all those can annoy me.

One day during the first year of our marriage, Philip told me that we should wash my car. Sounded like fun to me! He brought out the bucket filled with sudsy water, a few sponges to do the washing and a hose. The hose had a nozzle on the end that allowed water to be sprayed. I took one look at that hose, then grabbed it and sprayed Philip. It just seemed like the fun, spontaneous thing to do in that moment. I was fully prepared for him to get into the fun by throwing water at me too.

He did not quite see it that way. In fact, he was not happy.

What was he there to do? To wash the car.

I was there to play. Washing the car was secondary.

Anyone see a problem here?

We worked through that situation and many others. We have learned to value each other. And—this is important—to laugh. Not at each other but at some of the ways we are different.

Whether you have married someone who is similar to you with a lot of the same strengths and weaknesses (scary thought) or someone quite different from you, it takes a bit of effort to go from hating your differences to understanding them and eventually to valuing them.

Don't expect your spouse to be like you. I don't expect Philip to be Mr. Social. I know that after he's been at a function for a few hours, he's ready for some quiet time. I don't resent that about him; I just accept it. At the same time, he has no problem with my desire to be with people. He is not threatened by my friendships. Actually, he says that my focus on people has helped him include more people in our life.

We all have irreconcilable differences.

All of us.

They are not, as I mentioned earlier, so evident when we are in that brain-dead, euphoric, cloudy state of dating—or if they are obvious, we don't mind them. When Philip and I were dating, I loved the fact that his car was always clean and that he showed up on time. Eventually, however, I called his punctuality and need for order picky.

He loved my spontaneity and my carefree ability to make everything fun. In time, though, he saw them as careless and irresponsible.

Same personality traits—we just looked at them differently.

The journey we have made and continue to make is to look for the strengths and to forgive the weaknesses.

Recently Philip and I both spoke at a church. A few days later, the pastor was making some comments to both of us and laughingly said, "Wow, you are both so different in your energy levels and styles. I am impressed that you have stayed married!"

Not only have we stayed married, but we also actually like each other.

And if we can do it, so can you!

There are plenty of differences that can divide, but I encourage you to see your differences as bringing strength to the whole.

Yes, there are differences, but perhaps we need to focus on the places in which we are similar. If we continue to emphasize the things that are different, we can get frustrated or even think of the other person as wrong. So how about focusing on the areas in which you are the same?

Here's Philip's and my list:

- We both love God.
- We both love each other.
- We are both committed to our marriage.
- We both love our children.
- We both love building the church.
- We both love our friends.

- We both love playing with other people's babies.
- We both love to travel.
- We both love the beach.
- We both love to read.
- We both love to laugh.
- We both love sitting in coffee shops and people watching.
- We both like swimming in the ocean when it is warm.
- We both like getting massages.
- We both like to play in New York City.
- We both like living in Los Angeles.
- We both like going to conferences to learn.
- We both like to teach.
- We both like movies.
- We both like dogs.
- We both like Indian food.
- We both like Thai food.
- We both take a *lot* of vitamins.
- We both work out.
- We both pray for our children and their future spouses.
- We both will love our grandchildren.
- We both are committed to our friends.
- We both want to make a contribution to our city and world.
- We both are committed to helping the orphan.
- We both hate injustice against children.
- We both are determined to see the next generation fulfill its purpose.
- Ninety-nine percent of our DNA is the same.

We can get frustrated at our differences, or we can focus on what unites us. Make your own list.

_____
_____
_____
_____
_____
_____
_____
_____

If we are united, nothing is impossible.
The apostle Paul said it best:

I want you to think about how all this makes you more
significant, not less. A body isn't just a single part blown
up into something huge. It's all the different-but-similar
parts arranged and functioning together. If Foot said, "I'm
not elegant like Hand, embellished with rings; I guess I
don't belong to this body," would that make it so? If Ear
said, "I'm not beautiful like Eye, limpid and expressive;
I don't deserve a place on the head," would you want to
remove it from the body? If the body was all eye, how could
it hear? If all ear, how could it smell? As it is, we see that
God has carefully placed each part of the body right where
he wanted it.

But I also want you to think about how this keeps
your significance from getting blown up into self-impor-
tance. *For no matter how significant you are, it is only because of
what you are a* part *of.* An enormous eye or a gigantic hand
wouldn't be a body, but a monster. What we have is one
body with many parts, each its proper size and in its proper
place. No part is important on its own. Can you imagine
Eye telling Hand, "Get lost; I don't need you"? Or, Head
telling Foot, "You're fired; your job has been phased out"?
As a matter of fact, in practice it works the other way—the
"lower" the part, the more basic, and therefore necessary.
You can live without an eye, for instance, but not without a stomach. When it's a part of your own body you are
concerned with, it makes *no* difference whether the part is
visible or clothed, higher or lower. You give it dignity and
honor just as it is, without comparisons. If anything, you
have more concern for the lower parts than the higher.
If you had to choose, wouldn't you prefer good digestion
to full-bodied hair?

The way God designed our bodies is a model for understanding our lives together as a church: *every part dependent
on every other part,* the parts we mention and the parts we
don't, the parts we see and the parts we don't. If one part

hurts, every other part is involved in the hurt, and in the healing. *If one part flourishes, every other part enters into the exuberance* (1 Cor. 12:14-26, *THE MESSAGE*, emphasis added).

Think It Through

Women

1. What do you think about when you hear or see the term "irreconcilable differences"? Does every relationship have irreconcilable differences? What makes you think so?
2. One definition of "cultivate" means "to cherish." Do you *cherish* unity? Are you willing to do the hard work of cultivating unity with your husband? What are some practical ways that you and your husband can work toward unity?
3. How would it affect your marriage if you began to focus on the areas in which you and your husband are similar rather than on your differences? What things would it enable you to do?
4. Make a list of the ways in which you and your husband are different. Now write a list of all the ways in which you are similar. Keep this list close to you at all times! When differences arise, focus on the "similar" list.

Men

1. What do you think about when you hear or see the term "irreconcilable differences"? Does every relationship have irreconcilable differences? What makes you think so?
2. Remember the story about the Human Genome Project? It found that human beings, at the genetic level, are almost 99 percent identical—we are more alike than we are different. What realizations began to stir in your heart as you read this?
3. Our differences were designed to make us stronger, not to divide us—but differences can divide us unless we seek unity. How is your wife different from you? How are you different from her? How, in light of what you have read in this chapter, do these differences make you stronger together?

4. Jesus prayed in John 17:20-23 that we would all be one, even as He and the Father are one. What did He mean by this?

5. Make a list of the ways in which you and your wife are different. Now write a list of all the ways in which you are similar. Keep this list close to you at all times! When differences arise, focus on the "similar" list.

6

You Had Me at Hello

Philip

Love isn't blind, it just only sees what matters.
Anonymous

Love each other with genuine affection,
and take delight in honoring each other.
Romans 12:10, *NLT*

Dreams are magnetic and powerful.

The dreams of little girls are fragile. The dreams of women are crucial.

She dreams of being a doctor.

She dreams of having a family.

She dreams of being in ministry.

She dreams of helping the hurting.

A woman's dreams are vital to her heart.

A man's dreams are no less important. His dreams are important to his confidence and hope. Men often define *who they are* by *what they do*. Dismissing his dreams is a great way to break his soul. A man will invest in a relationship based on how he feels when he is around a woman.

He dreams of having his own business.

He dreams of being a pastor.

He dreams of having enough money in the bank to take care of his family.

He dreams of playing baseball or playing in the symphony.

One of the greatest dreams of every woman is the dream of being loved, truly loved, by a man who adores her—a man who cares more about her than he cares about his career. (Is that possible? Yes, it is.) She may also desire a man who is smarter, stronger and more handsome than any other. And women who love God want a man who has faith and is passionate about life.

But mostly girls dream about a man who will love, honor and be there for her. Women want someone they can trust at the deepest level!

In the movie *Jerry Maguire*, Tom Cruise plays the part of a sports agent. Jerry is struggling in his career to establish his own agency. In his attempt to make it, he is trying to sign the NFL receiver he represents to a big contract. This will establish him as a legitimate agent, validating his agency and securing his career as an independent agent.

His wife, Dorothy, helps to make it all happen, but Jerry focuses on his goal and loses sight of his relationship with her. He finally lands the contract, but he realizes that without the love of his life to share this moment, his victory means nothing.

Jerry goes to find Dorothy in order to repair the damage he has done through his neglect. He finds her in the living room, in a support-group meeting full of frustrated women who don't trust men so much anymore. He stands in front of all these women to declare his love for his wife. He attempts to describe how much he values her, how much he honors her and how meaningless his life is without her.

As he stumbles through his apologies, stutters through a description of his revelation, he begins expressing his love for her—right there in front of God and everybody.

I remember cringing in the theater during this scene. I get embarrassed for people when they are embarrassing themselves. I was worried. *Where is this going? Is he going to make this worse? Is she going to tell him to get out?*

But my anxiety was unnecessary, because he does a really great job!

Jerry goes on and on, saying all the honoring and loving things that should have been said long ago. But then Dorothy interrupts—she has heard enough!

"Shut up—just shut up. You had me at hello."

You had me at hello? How is that possible?

When a man tries to sincerely convey how much he loves a woman, when he is expressing from the heart the honor he feels for her, it can be felt beyond the words he speaks. Honoring is powerful. That kind of love is healing. It's engaging. That's it! That's the kind of love that every woman desires, the kind of loving honor that Dorothy had been waiting for. Every woman wants a man who will declare his love publicly before God, humanity and even a room full of the disillusioned. The heart of every woman in that living-room support group was touched, because the lack of loving honor is what brought each of them to that meeting in the first place.

Honor in the heart empowers the words that come out of the mouth. Jerry stands there, doing his best to honor Dorothy by expressing the depth of his love for her. And it's his willingness to do that—to honor her even in an embarrassing situation, putting his pride at risk—that touches her heart. That's why he has her at hello.

Ladies and gentlemen, we have a winner!

When a man hears his girlfriend, fiancée or wife talk about how impressed she is with his talents, skills or achievements, and when she brags on him in front of others, he is encouraged. He comes to life, and he believes that this woman is really brilliant in her ability to recognize skill.

Holly will sometimes say things like, "Philip is really a genius when it comes to . . ." Before she finishes her statement, I think, *What is that she is going to say? I gotta hear this.* I try to act like her words don't affect me. She exaggerates in most areas, but when she talks like this, she is fairly accurate. I think, *Maybe I am a genius in this area.*

I did fill out an application for Mensa once. It hasn't come back yet.

It's been four years. I may not get in.

That is what it feels like to be honored. Expressing genuine honor to someone is one of the most powerful components of a great relationship. To honor someone you love is to declare his or her value to you, to demonstrate your appreciation of that person and to express his or her importance to you in a way that is obvious to others.

Both men and women need to be honored. In fact, everyone needs to be honored. We are challenged in the Scripture to give honor to whom honor is due (see Rom. 13:7). Honor is the way healthy people and good people treat each other.

It is healthy for you to expect honor in relationships and in life. While you cannot demand honor from anyone, you can request it. It is important that you give honor to others as well; give, and it shall be given to you.

Men are very sensitive to the issue of honor. Women, are you respecting your husband? He will gravitate away from dishonor and toward honor. A man is as tender in his ego as a woman is in her feelings.

My intention in this book is to encourage you to be more effective in your ability to honor others.

Women, I want to present some ideas that could help you to have a great relationship with the man in your life. *I believe in you.*

Men, I want you to experience the power of honoring the woman in your life. The world needs you to shine in your marriage. We need you to flourish. Your family needs you to flourish. Your friends need you to overcome the battles you face. Your church needs your example of strength and determination. Our world needs your grace in relationships. Without what you bring to our world, life will be less than what is intended—for all of us.

God has a plan for women. They are important to God's plan. Women are important to men. They have an irreplaceable role.

Women are lovers, and they are leaders. They are encouragers, and they are friends. Women can turn the ordinary into the amazing. What a woman can do and who she is can bring out God's best in any situation.

If you want a great life, invite a woman whose light is shining into your world. There are many amazing women whose gifts are hidden from the rest of us, hidden because of wounds of the heart.

Women need to be loved and admired by the men who are important to them. They need honor in order to flourish—but too few have that experience. Some are ignored, some are disregarded, and many have their value overlooked. In the absence of admiration, a woman's uniqueness is too often hidden.

Some women suffer abuse. When this happens, not only is God's gifting not allowed to blossom in them, but also the light in them is put out. What God intended to be a light burning bright is reduced to a smoldering wick, a spiraling breath of smoke where a flame was intended.

Usually when I talk to a woman during her first two years of marriage, I see smiles, funny stories and a gleam in her eye. But on this day, sitting in my office, there was none of that. Sandy sat in an awkward silence, trying to work up the strength to describe her marriage while keeping her composure. Her moist eyes revealed pain. It seemed hard for her to breathe.

Silence often speaks louder than words.

"Where do I start? We were so in love. I don't know what happened. He seems like a different man. Everything was great in the beginning, but we have grown apart so quickly. I feel like I'm suffocating. I guess I married the wrong person. I wish I knew how to go back to what we had."

This is a familiar story. It is repeated in various forms. The names change, but the situations are recognizable.

"I love him," she continued. "But I don't know how much longer I can do this. I feel like we are just roommates who can't agree on much. He never touches me, he doesn't hold me—unless he wants sex. And that is not often. I've lost respect for him, and I don't trust him anymore. What can we do?"

Do you know someone in that situation? Have you been there? Perhaps we can define a road that will lead to life in our relationships. Let's take a look. Maybe we can discover a path that will lead us back to the love that brought us together.

Men need to be admired, appreciated and encouraged. When those things disappear from a relationship, life begins to drain out of a man's heart quickly.

"I feel like she tolerates me. When we were first married," Jim said, "she admired me, but now I feel like I can't do anything right. How could so much change in two years?"

Women, if you want to reengage the man in your life, inject a healthy portion of honor back into your relationship.

Five Qualities of a Thriving Relationship

What does it take to have a great relationship? In this day and age,
is it even possible anymore? I want to offer some suggestions that
I believe can help create a great relationship.

The ultimate human relationship is marriage. Holly and I have
been married for 29 years. We have had many struggles and challenges, but we have a great relationship today. I have also coached
others on their marriages. I've seen people turn their lifeless or
disappointing marriages around. What looked like relationships
headed for a train wreck became fulfilling and wonderful part-
nerships. I have learned some things in the last 29 years that I
know make a marriage great. I'm almost certain we will make it
to 30 years!

If you truly desire to have a great marriage, let me assure you
that it *is* possible. If you are single and still looking for "the one,"
please take the next few pages very seriously. If you are married
and want to rekindle your passion into a lasting love, the following
are some practical steps you can take to lead the way. If you want
to enjoy a relationship based on the love you've always dreamed
about, please consider these five qualities of a thriving relationship. If your relationship lacks one or more of these qualities,
don't worry—we'll also explore how to develop each of these components in your relationship.

The First Quality of a Thriving Relationship: Honor

If you are single and evaluating whether someone will make a good
mate, start here:

- Does he or she show honor to others?
- Is it difficult for him or her to show respect for others?
- Does he or she express honor to you?
- Does this person honor your desires, your goals and your
  boundaries? Or does he or she often disregard what is
  important to you?
- Does he or she try to talk you out of the standards that
  establish your values?
- Does this person push you to change your dreams to
  accommodate his or her own desires?

If you are married and wondering what's missing in your marriage, it may be honor. If you want to breathe some life back into a stalled relationship, add a dash of genuine honor to your marital recipe.

Demonstrate how important your spouse is to you by honoring him—his strengths, his goals and his feelings. Recognize her fears and the circumstances and situations that make her insecure, and accept these things instead of criticizing. Allow him or her to express boundaries, and leave some room for your spouse to grow and change. Accept your husband or wife's likes and dislikes because you accept and admire him or her.

Honor the man or woman in your life. Honor is powerful. That kind of love is healing. It's engaging. And it's the kind of love every person desires.

Women must realize that men are not their enemy, they are their ally. I have been strong in advocating that women be honored, celebrated and empowered in their gifts and leadership. But be careful that in your effort to be strong and free, you are not so strong that you ignore your husband and shut down the men in your world with cries of "I am woman, and it's *my* turn now." This will not lead you to a place of freedom but to heartbreak and frustration.

As we saw with Jerry and Dorothy, honor in the heart empowers the words that come out of the mouth. Expressing honor to someone is one of the most powerful components of a great relationship. Honor unexpressed is completely irrelevant.

A great way to express honor is to communicate admiration. Verbalize your acceptance of your spouse; express how and why you value him or her, and demonstrate your respect for something within your husband or wife: his vision, her dreams, his incredible work ethic, the way she loves your children. When you do, there's a good chance that you'll bring new life to your relationship.

If your spouse were Jesus, how would you treat him or her?

"What?" you may say. "That's a little extreme, don't you think?"

Well, maybe. But when you honor others, it does bring out something special in them *that criticism never will*.

What famous person would you like to meet? Who is impressive to you?

I once got to meet Michael Jordan in person. You have to realize that MJ was a hero to me. I loved watching him play basketball. I enjoyed hearing about his story on and off the court. In my opinion, he was a once-in-a-lifetime basketball player. He was bigger than the team; he was bigger than the sport. Followers of the game still compare the best players of today to MJ. I think they always will.

When Jordan was filming the movie *Space Jam*, he had a temporary gym erected in a large tent on a back lot in Burbank. Some friends of mine had access to the tent and invited me there for a pick-up game of basketball with some local college and NBA players. Between games I was introduced to Jordan; we shook hands and exchanged a casual greeting.

Are you kidding me? I just met Michael Jordan! I tried to look very cool on the outside, but on the inside I was pumped! I told everyone about that moment. It was such an honor to meet my hero. I admired him.

That was several years ago, and he doesn't call me anymore. Actually, he never called me. I never see him. Basically, I have no relationship with him. But meeting him made me realize that I could easily express more honor for MJ than I sometimes express for my own wife. I recognized that I needed to put some of that enthusiastic honor into my relationship with Holly.

Whom do you admire? Whom would you most like to meet? Maybe you would name a celebrity like Denzel Washington, Will Smith, Taylor Swift or Julia Roberts. Would you like to meet a famous businessperson, such as Microsoft founder Bill Gates, Larry Page or Sergey Brin, the founders of Google, or Howard Schultz, founder of Starbucks? Maybe you'd like to meet a famous politician—the president of the United States, a former president or a famous senator. Or you might pick a well-known sports personality like Derek Jeter, LeBron James or Venus Williams.

Who is that someone who could make you gush with admiring words? It seems like a natural response to react that way to someone famous, but it's actually much more important that we honor those we love—particularly the one we're building a life with.

Early in our marriage, Holly would come to me and express feelings of hurt or frustration. She would say, "I feel like you just don't care about me." And I'd just get mad.

I am pretty sure there's only one thing you are not supposed to say when your wife comes to you with words like Holly did. Naturally, that one thing is exactly what I said: "What? That's crazy! You shouldn't feel like that!"

Did that help the situation? No. Did it bring us closer? No. Think Vesuvius or Mount St. Helens, and you have an idea where those conversations went. Note to self: *If you want to push your wife toward the possibility of going postal, disregard her feelings.*

Then I tried just saying nothing. Still she would get heated. "What?" I'd respond defensively. "I didn't say anything."

To which she would reply, "Yeah, but it's the way you aren't saying it."

I do love my wife, and I do care about what she feels. I don't always understand what she feels—but that is not a good reason for me to withhold honor from her. Our whole rapport changed when I learned how to respond to a comment like "I feel like I'm a bother to you." I learned to respond to her concerns with genuine concern, to sincerely communicate that I care: "I'm so sorry you feel that way. That must feel horrible. I'm sorry if I've done anything to make you feel like that. I never want anything I do to cause you to feel that way. What do you think I can do, even if we don't agree right now, that would make you feel loved and appreciated?"

Wow—completely different results!

I suggest that you put some effort into honoring the person who looks to you for love and respect. Honor him with some of the same passion you would show to a celebrity with whom you will probably never have a relationship. Don't wait for your spouse to take the lead—set the example by expressing your admiration. Without a daily injection of honor, every relationship begins to die just a little every day.

The Second Quality of a Thriving Relationship: Communication

Communication is *the* golden key to a great relationship. Good communication is about knowing what to say, how to say it and when to say it. No easy task. It takes work.

Most men communicate differently than women.

Even though this is a generalization, most men need to learn to communicate better. But let me say this to the women: no matter how good at communicating a man becomes, he will likely never communicate like a woman.

I think many a woman secretly thinks that if her husband improves in his communication ability, he will communicate more like her girlfriends.

Not going to happen!

I'll say more about these differences later in this chapter. But remember this: Not only is your spouse different from you, but they will be different from you for the rest of your life.

She may communicate to convey a feeling or to paint a picture. He may communicate to get a point across or to convey information. And men speak differently when they feel that they are going to lose status by admitting an error. Communicate your disagreements to a man not in order to blame him or to make him feel wrong but to let him know how he can be an even greater hero.

I'm sitting down to dinner with Holly, and she says, "Did you do that errand I asked you to do today?"

Simple enough question.

"Yes. Well, what errand? Oh, man, I forgot. Can I get it tomorrow?"

"I needed you to do it today. Why didn't you pick it up? You said you would. I should have just done it myself."

"I'm really sorry I forgot it. I can't—"

"What did you do today? I feel as if what I need is not important to you."

"You know, weirdly enough, my leg is falling asleep right now. I need to stand up and walk around a bit," I blurt out.

It wasn't a total lie. I was experiencing some tingling sensations, but mostly they were in my stomach, because I was afraid that I was going to feel even more like an idiot in the next two minutes than I did right then.

I like the conversations that go like this: I admit a mistake I made, and my wife says, "I appreciate your honesty and that you are willing to talk to me about this. A lot of women have husbands who lie to them."

Yay. I admit a wrong, and I get props on it. "Well, let's talk again anytime you want."

Are you at a standstill in your relationship? What are you communicating? What does your spouse think you are conveying that weakens your relationship?

Are you considering a relationship with someone who is not a very good communicator? That is a dangerous decision. The person you allow to get involved with your heart needs to see the importance of communication, have the desire to communicate and be willing to improve in that area.

There are no other good options.

A person who is not willing to communicate or to learn how to communicate is basically giving up the quality of their relationship to chance.

Years ago I had a friend who became discouraged about our friendship. He thought I did not care about him as a person, and in fact he said something to me like, "I don't think you care much about me."

I asked him if he remembered the times I had invited him places or the times I had asked him how he was doing or how he was feeling.

He said that he didn't think I had meant it.

"Well, help me understand," I said. "I invited you to meet me for coffee or go to a movie several times. Why didn't you let me know some of your concerns or feelings in those moments?"

"I didn't think you were interested," he said.

This shows a major communication breakdown. If we don't say something, how can we expect a situation to change? If we don't convey our feelings or fears, how can we hold a person accountable to our expectations?

Sometimes we think we are communicating one thing, but we are not—we are communicating something totally different than what we thought.

Once Holly and I were walking together. We were enjoying each other's presence. It was quiet. I loved the simplicity of having my wife with me, of walking, of taking in the beauty and the sounds around us. We were reflecting on the connection we shared.

That's what I thought we were doing.

Holly said, "What are you thinking? Why are you so quiet?"

"We're enjoying the moment together." I admit now that I was sort of guessing on that.

"I want to know how you feel about our relationship."

"Have you ever heard that love song from the movie *Notting Hill* that goes 'You say it best when you say nothing at all'?" I said sincerely.

"That's a guys' song! That was totally written by a guy," she clarified.

"Oh. I thought it was romantic."

"Sometimes it can be. But right now I want to hear how you feel about me."

I decided not to mention the other song that came to mind. The one by the 80s group Extreme, "More Than Words": "Then you wouldn't have to say that you love me 'cause I'd already know."

"I feel—hungry."

She looked at me. "That's not a feeling."

"Oh, right."

All of us communicate in words and tone. We communicate with our attitudes and our body posture. Often we think that we are saying one thing, but in reality we are communicating something else. We say one thing with our words and another with our actions. We say one thing with our attitude and another with our words. I think we just don't pay attention.

Work on communicating clearly and effectively.

There are a few essentials that must be sought after and conveyed by both people in a relationship if intimacy is to result: *interests, expectations, appreciation, encouragement* and *commitment* all need to be communicated clearly and passionately.

Sit down and talk. Listen first. Really listen. Then tell your story. *Communicate your interests.* Share what fascinates you. Talk about what you love so much that you want to do it for the rest of your life. What makes you feel alive? What makes you smile from the heart?

What bores you? What do you hate so much that you will probably never change your opinion about it? What things have you disliked at one point in your life that you grew to enjoy later? What do you dislike but may be able to accept if it is important to someone you love?

Communicate your expectations. Expectations must be talked out. Sometimes, when we do this, we discover that we have unrealistic expectations about people, marriage or life. We can save ourselves a lot of frustration by releasing these unrealistic expectations.

Sometimes we may describe an expectation that we hold and find that our partner is unable or unwilling to meet that expectation. Then we have important relationship decisions to make.

What do you expect from marriage?

What do you believe a husband or wife should do or be?

What does your life need to look like in five years in order for you to be happy?

What do you expect from God, from yourself and from life?

Communicate your appreciation. Expressing appreciation brings you and your spouse together. It causes defenses to melt away. Tell your husband or wife that you appreciate his or her efforts, actions, attempts and strengths.

Tell her that you appreciate it when she says_____.

That you don't like it when he doesn't say _____.

Tell the other person that you appreciate the gift he or she gave you.

Tell your spouse the 10 things about him or her that you are grateful for.

Tell him or her that you notice the sacrifices he or she has made and how much that means to you.

Tell your husband or wife the qualities of character that you see, admire and appreciate in him or her.

Post a Twitter or Facebook update or an Instagram photo about how awesome your spouse is, and let the whole world know!

Most women like to be with a man who makes her feel safe and secure; most men tend to love a woman because of how he feels about himself when he is with her. It is a major mistake to make a man feel inadequate or uncertain, to make him feel that he is always auditioning or always wrong. Communicating appreciation tells a man that you respect him. When your husband feels that you genuinely respect him, trust increases.

I believe that one bad comment can wipe out 20 positive acts of kindness. Bad comments happen, so make sure that you overdose on the appreciation. Convey respect for *who your spouse is* and *what he or she feels.* When you communicate appreciation for what your spouse does, thinks and needs, he or she will trust you.

Communicate your encouragement. Encourage her for taking risks.

Encourage his attempts at being a loving father and husband.

Encourage her efforts toward improving her health.

Encourage his dependability and the provision that he contributes to your family.

Encourage her spiritual hunger, his personal growth or her efforts to strengthen your relationship.

Encourage each other's accomplishments or achievements.

Encouragement and recognition are so important to a man. Don't forget to give them. Affirm what he has done and encourage him in what he would like to do. And men, affirmation to your wife will let her know that you notice her and that you care.

This kind of treatment will always build bridges and break down walls.

Communicate your commitment. One of the most powerful and reassuring messages about Jesus is the biblical promise, "Never will I leave you; never will I forsake you" (Heb. 13:5). That is a commitment. His last words to His followers, according to Matthew, were, "I am with you always, to the very end of the age" (Matt. 28:20). Jesus knew how to communicate commitment.

Commitment is powerful. That's why the wedding is so important: it is the vow we make—our commitment before God, family and friends. *Through times of sickness and times of health, through good times or bad, I'm committed to you.*

In the middle of a debate or argument, try communicating your commitment. Interject a reassurance about your commitment to the relationship; you'll find that commitment calms the fears of the soul.

The Third Quality of a Thriving Relationship: Patience

Things change. People change. Patience is the quality that allows us to gain understanding of these changes. It enables us to allow one another to get it wrong occasionally without being thrown out of the game. Two of the most valuable commodities for marriage are flexibility and adaptability, and these are perfected through patience.

Patience allows other positive qualities a chance to emerge. Kindness is a fruit of the Spirit; in other words, kindness is evidence that God is working in our heart. It takes patience to be kind, because if we want to avoid our immediate reactions like "What were you thinking?!" we must be willing to delay our response.

Patience also allows time for our perspective to be adjusted.

This perspective change was so crucial for Holly and me. We are so different in so many ways, and it would have been easier for us in the early days to give up. We would wonder, *How is this going to work?*

She is extremely cheerful and energetic—*all* the time! She makes normal people look depressed.

"Why are they so sad?" she asks.

"They are not sad; you are just—unusually happy. You don't realize that you are not normal."

Back then I found her energy and excitement a little too much and a lot tiring. But over time I have gained a new perspective. My wife's enthusiasm is contagious. She brings joy to everyone around her.

We have to change our perspective about our differences, or they can bury us. We can focus on our differences as a problem, or we can see them as assets that build our team. We can focus on weaknesses or on strengths. Patience allows us the option to choose where we will put our focus.

The Fourth Quality of a Thriving Relationship: Follow-through

When you depend on someone who does what he says he will do, it is easy to trust him. And when you trust your spouse, your relationship can continue to go forward even when setbacks occur in your life.

Follow-through is important for many athletic skills, such as serving in tennis, shooting in basketball or swinging a baseball bat. The observant coach, when he or she sees a breakdown in follow-through, can often help a player get back lost strength. A golfer's swing gets better results and a bowler sees his ball back in the zone when follow-through is corrected.

Follow through on the little things, and follow through on the big things. Dependability is relationship glue.

Many relationships get weaker and weaker because trust has eroded.

"I just can't trust her anymore."

"He never does what he says he'll do."

Marriage can recover missing trust with an admission that you've dropped the ball or let the other down. A renewed dedication to follow-through is reassuring. Working less, spending time with the kids or being more careful with the budget are areas that all matter—but the central issue is follow-through—taking responsibility for your contributions, outcomes and mistakes.

"Many claim to have unfailing love, but a faithful person who can find?" (Prov. 20:6). If you are single, don't expect the undependable person you are dating to suddenly become Mr. Follow-Through two minutes after he says, "I do." If he is not dependable before the wedding, he won't magically become dependable after it.

Paul concludes his direction for marriage in Ephesians by summing it up this way: "Each one of you [husbands] also must love his wife as he loves himself, and the wife must respect her husband" (Eph. 5:33).

We all need love, and we all need respect, but there is something about the priorities of love for a woman and respect for a man. I picture the image of pedaling a bicycle to demonstrate the momentum that is possible in this dynamic. Pushing one pedal down brings the other one up. Push the other pedal down, and it brings the first one up. Keep that up, and you have momentum. In marriage, the husband expresses and demonstrates love to his wife, which inspires in her respect. The wife demonstrates respect toward her husband, which empowers and motivates him to express genuine love. Keep that up, and you have momentum.

Will you be someone who will follow through? Is the man or woman you are considering building your life with a person who will follow through?

We must continue, no matter the circumstances, to follow through on love and respect. In every marriage that stalls out, breaks up or goes through a rough patch, the husband stops loving his wife as she needs, and the wife stops respecting her husband as he needs. Each one stops following through with the important ingredient he or she adds to the relationship.

To get the momentum going again, he must love her like she's the most important person in the world. She must show respect and admiration for him. That is the follow-through that is essential. I've seen this simple adjustment transform a relationship completely.

The Fifth Quality of a Thriving Relationship: Humility

Humility may be the most difficult character quality to develop—which is a little bit funny, since it shouldn't take much of it to realize that we are all flawed, that we can't get it right all the time. Humility is the willingness to admit failure.

Humble people demonstrate a desire to grow. A humble husband or wife is willing to learn to recognize his or her spouse's needs. Humility affords us the ability to yield to the needs of the other rather than focus wholly on our own. Humility also values the victories of others, even when victory is far removed from us. The humble are forgiving, releasing others from IOUs that steal the life out of relationships.

A humble man apologizes, forgives and prays for the ability to love his bride the way Christ loves the church. A humble woman expresses respect to her husband in a way that builds trust in his heart. She is willing to discover genuine interest in things that matter to him.

Dr. Phil, the self-help author and TV host, says, "Sometimes you make the right decision, sometimes you make the decision right." When we make a poor decision, it requires humility to admit it and to correct it. Humility demands that we make the situation right by doing the right thing.

Pride kills relationships, and humility is the only antidote for pride. James encourages us, "Humble yourselves before the Lord, and he will lift you up" (Jas. 4:10).

These five qualities are just a few that build great relationships. Each one has the potential to restore joy, love and trust to the most broken of relationships.

Think It Through

Women

1. "Men need to be admired, appreciated and encouraged. When those things disappear from a relationship, life begins to drain out of a man's heart quickly." How do you show honor in your relationship with your husband? How do you like honor shown to you?

2. Remember, a man will never communicate the way your girlfriends do. How can you be understanding of the differences between you and your husband and supportive of his communication style as a man?

3. How patient are you? Could you be more flexible and adaptable in the areas in which your husband is different from you? Make a list of areas in which you could exercise patience toward your husband. Pick one, and put it into practice today.

4. How about follow-through? How good are you at doing what you say you're going to do? One of the biggest ways we can follow through with our men is to keep on respecting them, on good days and on tough days.

5. Humility is the willingness to admit failure. Have you ever been afraid to admit that you were wrong about something? How would your husband respond if you chose humility regarding some issue that you disagree on?

Men

1. "Women need to be loved and admired by the men who are important to them. They need honor in order to flourish." How do you show honor in your relationship with your wife? How do you like honor shown to you?

2. How can you communicate your interests, expectations, appreciation, encouragement and commitment to your wife clearly and effectively? In which one of these areas can you make a deliberate effort to communicate to your wife this week? Will you do it?

3. Patience with others helps us to adjust our perspective of them. How can being patient with your wife give you a fresh point of view on who she is as a person?
4. Follow-through brings strength to a relationship, because the result is trust. Why?
5. What are some of the qualities of a humble person? How could cultivating humility in your relationship with your wife strengthen your marriage?

7

Sleeping with the Enemy

Holly

> If you have only one smile in you, give it to the people you love.
> Don't be surly at home, then go out in the street and start grinning
> "Good morning" at total strangers.
> Maya Angelou

> If a house is divided against itself, that house cannot stand.
> Mark 3:25

> What causes fights and quarrels among you? Don't they come
> from your desires that battle within you?
> James 4:1

"This was your idea."

"No, it was yours. I wanted to go yesterday."

"Why are you always blaming me?"

"You never listen to me!"

"You never do what I want anyway!"

She goes and slams the door.

Sounds like a couple of children, doesn't it? But this is an argument I overheard between two adults.

Most of us enter into marriage with great intentions and not many skills. So many marriages fail because people aren't willing to develop the necessary skills.

Conflicts in marriage *will* arise, because we are not clones who think and act alike all the time. These conflicts can be used to strengthen or to destroy. Learning to handle conflict that rises inside and outside a marriage is crucial to the long-term health and wholeness of the relationship.

Conflict in marriage is different from conflict on the battlefield. Your spouse is not your enemy—even though it feels that way sometimes! Destroying your spouse, whether through hateful words, indifference or neglect, will destroy you. Because the two of you are one.

I had a discussion one time with a woman who said that she and her husband never argued; conflict never arose in their marriage. As I spent time with them, I noticed that this was basically true. I also noticed a total lack of intimacy and honesty and a superficial level of communication that would eventually lead to trouble or boredom. Allowing and resolving conflict keeps lines of communication open and gives each spouse an opportunity to air his or her differences.

The apostle James tells us that most of our conflicts occur because of selfishness. "I want what I want, and I want it now, and you want what you want." When those desires compete, we have conflict.

Wouldn't it be easier if life were like the climate control in a car? The car Philip and I have has dual controls, so I can make it cooler or warmer on my side of the car, and Philip can have his side how he wants it. I can even warm up my car seat, and he can make his cool. Pretty awesome! Sometimes I wish life was full of his-and-her everything, but it isn't. Most of the time, the conflict we experience in marriage arises because we are not willing to give up what we want.

I have a friend who was raised in a family whose way to resolve any conflict was to fight it out. Just fight until you win. They didn't necessarily physically fight, but they definitely had verbal fights that got louder and louder. One person always had to win, and the other was made to feel totally wrong. There was either complete domination or complete submission—no compromising or meeting in the middle.

Surely this is not the best way.

I have also talked to people raised in families in which one of the parents always backed down from anything resembling a confrontation. One or both parents just gave in so they could avoid any conflict whatsoever. One of my friends who grew up in such an environment told me that this method of resolving conflict kept the peace for a while but that eventually there was an inevitable explosion.

This way can't be good either.

There are right and wrong ways to face and resolve conflict.

I am not a big fan of boxing, but I do know that there are rules in boxing. In karate, there are rules. In wrestling, there are rules. I am not sure about the WWF or *Lucha Libre* (made famous in the movie *Nacho Libre*), but I suspect that even in those matches there are rules of some kind.

The first rule of conflict is to make sure that you are, personally, at peace with God.

It sounds so basic.

We are created to have relationship with God, and all our ability to connect with people comes out of our relationship with Him. I don't think that we can ever have peace with people if we haven't made our peace with God. Sometimes conflict occurs because we are expecting people—in this case, our spouse—to meet needs that only God can meet. We explored this idea more deeply in an earlier chapter. As amazing as Philip is—and most days he is amazing—he is not my Savior. He has nothing with which to save me. I must make peace with God rather than expecting Philip to make everything okay.

And in our relationship with God, we need to talk to Him about whatever issue or conflict we are dealing with—our children, work, finances, whatever. Even the simple things, but especially those conflicts that we think might get a little heated between our spouse and us. Talk to God about it *first. Pray first.* I wasn't always great at this; or if I did talk to God about my problems, it was more like whining. Something like, "You made this lunatic I am married to. *You* fix him!" That is not the talking-to-God I am talking about.

Ask God just how much of the problem might be your fault. Before you attack or accuse or blame, check yourself out. Jesus said that before we worry about that little piece of sawdust in somebody else's eye, we should remove the tree trunk from our own (see Matt. 7:3-5). And we *all* have tree trunks in our own eyes sometimes. Yet we can get so focused on the weaknesses and faults of the other that we forget we have them. The reality is that whatever part of a conflict is my fault is 100 percent my fault. I have to own that.

So now I ask myself questions such as, *Am I being oversensitive? Am I being insensitive? Am I being ungrateful or too demanding?* Oftentimes, if I am honest, the answer to one of those is yes. And I am 100 percent responsible for my part.

Here is the tough part. Apologize for your part of the problem first.

Get great at saying "I'm sorry."

Not "I'm sorry, but . . ."

Just "I'm sorry for being oversensitive" or for being too demanding or whatever.

I am sure that your spouse needs to apologize too. Your husband or wife has a tree trunk in his or her eye too. But you can only deal with you. Be 100 percent responsible for your part.

Get great at saying "I'm sorry." Because maybe, just maybe, you are wrong in this instance.

Fresh Perspective

I can only see in the direction my eyes are facing. I can't see behind me unless I turn my head. People behind me can tell me if my shirt is untucked or if there is a string hanging from the bottom of my skirt, but the direction my eyes are facing is the only perspective I have.

Likewise, each of us can only see life from our own perspective. And that means we all have the potential to be wrong in any given situation. Maybe in a particular instance I am wrong. I could be—and the more I am willing to say or simply acknowledge that likelihood, the more I pave the way toward building trust with my spouse. And trust is the goal.

Even at work or with friends, I have found that if someone is willing to admit a fault or a wrong, then the heart of that person is a heart I can work with. It is a heart I can partner with. Too many times we think that saying "I'm sorry" or "I'm wrong" might make us look bad. No, it won't. It will make us look strong. It takes a strong person to look at himself or herself and say, "I am so sorry; I was oversensitive in that moment."

Apologizing does not mean that the issue is over; it just means that the right atmosphere now exists for solving whatever the conflict is.

Trying to see an issue from the other's point of view is important. This is not always easy, because again, we only see life from our own perspective. A number of years ago, Philip and I were looking for a house to buy. This was when I was still living under the illusion that all men knew how to fix things or at least knew how to manage people who knew how to fix things. We walked into a house that was for sale. It was the funkiest house ever. I just loved it. It had a tree growing right in the middle of it. The previous owner had begun some renovations and had laid the groundwork for what I thought would be the most amazing house ever.

As I walked around the place, I was saying things like, "We could put this here and do that there. In this room we could do this." But as Philip walked through it, he saw all the work that would need to be done—none of which he knew how to do. In his mind he saw months of sawdust, hammers and chaos.

As he let me know that there was no way we were going to live in that house, I got frustrated. I said things like, "Why do we always have to do things your way? Why can't we have a house like this?"

I remember walking off by myself, taking a few deep breaths and really trying to see it from his perspective. He wanted a home. A peaceful home. He had no idea how to create a peaceful home out of this half-finished building. I saw the stress that even the thought of living here gave him.

So we walked away from that house that needed lots of work, and eventually we moved into a beautiful home that only required us to unpack our boxes and hang a lamp. Perfect! My working hard at trying to see the issue from my husband's point of view helped resolve that particular conflict.

Time and Place

Pick a good time to resolve the issue. Timing is key. Take it from me: on the way to your husband's birthday party is probably *not* the time to let him know that he could stand to lose a few pounds. (Wish I could tell you I learned that from a book!) Now the issue might be a fair one to bring up, but the timing is not good.

Maybe your wife's mom just got diagnosed with Alzheimer's. This is not the time to tell her that you think she should read a book on parenting. Again, the issue is a fair one to bring up—it's just that the timing is wrong.

The book of Esther tells the story of an ordinary girl who chose to live an extraordinary life. She was orphaned, raised by her uncle and, as a Jew in Persia, lived in a community of marginalized people. But ultimately, she was selected by the king to be his queen. What a fairy tale! Now Esther was living on easy street. She could have just kicked back and enjoyed her life of royalty and leisure—and she probably did for a while. But then she found out that her husband's right-hand man had devised a plan to kill all the Jews.

What was she going to do?

Esther's uncle told her that she had a responsibility to go to the king and ask him to override the evil man's plans. At first Esther was hesitant to do this, knowing that doing so could cost her life; anyone approaching the king uninvited could be put to death. But then she realized that maybe rescuing her people was the very reason she had been entrusted with her royal position. Maybe being queen wasn't just so she could enjoy luxury. Maybe she was in this position so that she could be a part of ending injustice. (Just a side thought here: I think you have been entrusted with this time in history and with your royal position so that, like Esther, you can be a part of ending injustice.)

Esther made the decision to approach the king. He didn't kill her. In fact, he asked what he could do for her.

What's interesting to me is that rather than telling him then and there about the plot to kill her people, Esther asked her husband to a banquet that she would prepare. Why didn't she just bring up the issue? I guess there was something about the time that didn't seem right.

The king enjoyed himself at the banquet and once again asked Esther what he could do for her. She told him that it would be great if he would come to another banquet the next night. What? Why didn't she just get to the point? I have no idea. But I think there must have been something about the timing.

At the banquet the next night, Esther told the king—very humbly yet directly—about the plot devised by his right-hand man to kill her and her people. The king was appalled, and he did everything in his power to see that Esther and her people were protected.

The conflict was resolved.

Esther was sensitive to the timing involved in resolving the conflict. There were times she could have said something but didn't.

I am not sure why waiting was a better option. But Esther's example made me realize that even when an issue I am dealing with is at the forefront of my mind, I still need to be sensitive about whether now is the right time to bring it up. The goal is to resolve the issue, not create another one.

Timing is important in conflict resolution, and so is place. Running out the door on the way to somewhere is probably not the right place to resolve anything. Neither my husband nor me will feel as if we are being heard, and both of us will feel that we need to hurry. The place to work out an issue is away from the telephone and from other distractions.

The bed is probably not the place to work out the issue either, because any man left horizontal for long will start snoring. (I didn't learn this from a book either. When Philip fell asleep in the middle of my sharing of an issue, it just created another issue we needed to deal with!) And the truth is, I don't want our bed to be a place of conflict. It should be a place for intimacy. I don't want to bring a fight there.

I am not opposed to a husband and wife having a disagreement in front of their children, as long as it is not an intense one, it is handled appropriately and the children see their parents resolve the conflict in a mature way. If the children only see their parents fight, slam doors and go their own way, then that negative picture is the one they will have of conflict. Too many times parents have a full-on, fully engaged, inappropriate attacking fight in front of their children—and the children, understandably, are freaked out. They're watching the people whom they are supposed to look to for guidance, wisdom and strength totally lose it. And that is a scary thing for children. Maybe the parents will resolve their issue behind closed doors a few hours later, but that does not help their children.

Taking a walk can be a great place for Philip and me to resolve issues. Or over coffee at Starbucks. Or sitting by the beach.

Or walking through the woods. Or at a park bench. You pick a place that works for you.

Rules of Engagement

So there is a time and a place—and there is a *how*.

Remember that the reason we have set aside a time and a place is to resolve our issue, so we need to come ready to do that. This is not the time to blame. This is not about *his* problem or *her* problem. We are married. This is *our* problem. We are on the same team. Sometimes, in the middle of a heated conflict, it is easy to forget that and to begin to point fingers. There have been times when I have felt as if I have won an argument, but I have brought damage to our relationship. Winning is not the goal. A strong relationship is.

Often Philip and I don't see eye to eye. (By now this is probably not a surprise to you.) But we are both committed to working out our problems together. Some days it is messier than others.

In films I have heard a soldier ask his superior officer what the rules of a particular engagement are. In other words, how and with what weapons should he fight? In marriage conflicts there must be rules of engagement. There are some very basic rules, ones you probably learned in kindergarten: No yelling. No pushing. No hitting. No kicking. No biting. No slamming doors.

In addition to those basics, I am going to give you a few of Philip's and mine—you can feel free to use these, or you can come up with your own. Whatever you decide, it is important that you and your spouse agree on them so that in the heat of a moment, you don't go with what you're feeling but instead stick to the rules you have decided on together.

Watch That Mouth!

Let no foul or polluting language, nor evil word nor unwholesome or worthless talk [ever] come out of your mouth, but only such [speech] as is good and beneficial to the spiritual progress of others, as is fitting to the need and the occasion, that it may be a blessing and give grace

(God's favor) to those who hear it. . . . Let all bitterness and indignation and wrath (passion, rage, bad temper) and resentment (anger, animosity) and quarreling (brawling, clamor, contention) and slander (evil-speaking, abusive or blasphemous language) be banished from you, with all malice (spite, ill will, or baseness of any kind). And become useful and helpful and kind to one another, tenderhearted (compassionate, understanding, loving-hearted), forgiving one another [readily and freely], as God in Christ forgave you (Eph. 4:29,31-32, *AMP*).

Think about the damage you might inflict before you launch that verbal missile. Sadly, sometimes my method is ready, fire, aim. Not good, and it can cause damage impossible to fix. Words cannot be taken back, only forgiven.

I love M&Ms®, especially the peanut ones. Back when I used to eat that kind of stuff, I could eat one bag in about 35 seconds—35 seconds to polish off a bag of fat, sugar and calories and about 30 minutes of exercise to work it off. Not to mention the hours that my body required to get rid of the toxins in it.

This is like a verbal missile: We can throw a hurtful word in a matter of seconds, but it may take years to work it off.

There once was a little boy who had a bad temper. His father gave him a bag of nails and told him that every time he lost his temper, he must hammer a nail into the back of the fence.

The first day the boy had driven 37 nails into the fence. Over the next few weeks, as he learned to control his anger, the number of nails hammered daily gradually dwindled down.

He discovered it was easier to hold his temper than to drive those nails into the fence.

Finally the day came when the boy didn't lose his temper at all. He told his father about it, and the father suggested that the boy now pull out one nail for each day that he was able to hold his temper.

The days passed, and the young boy was finally able to tell his father that all the nails were gone.

The father took his son by the hand and led him to the fence. He said, "You have done well, my son, but look at the holes in the fence. The fence will never be the same. When you say things in anger, they leave a scar just like this one. You can put a knife in a man and draw it out. It won't matter how many times you say I'm sorry, the wound is still there."

A verbal wound is as bad as a physical one.[1]

Most of the time we are kinder and more polite to strangers and acquaintances than we are to our spouse. It should not be that way, but often it is. Little acts of kindness can go a long way toward diffusing conflict. I never feel like being courteous or kind when Philip and I are disagreeing; I feel like criticizing, blaming and generally being anything but kind. But if I do choose to be kind or courteous, the conflict can be diffused. I can throw water or oil on the flame. It is up to me.

There are some verbal weapons that Philip and I have agreed will never be launched. We have decided that no matter what kind of conflict we get into, we will never use the word "divorce." Ever. If divorce is not an option, then working the conflict out is the only solution.

We try to refrain from using words like "never" and "always," because they are rarely true. "You *never* do anything I want to do!" "You *always* ignore me!" "You *never* think of me!" "You *never* say that you love me!"

Nobody "always" or "never" does anything, so be careful about using these absolute words.

It is better to express feelings using the expression "I feel . . ."

"I feel lonely or worried when you don't call me on the phone."

"I feel hurt when you talk about me to other people."

"I feel sad when you ignore me."

And it is important that we each own our own feelings; the other person is not responsible for how we feel. Using the expression "I feel . . ." is better than "You made me feel . . ." because nobody can *make* you feel anything.

One issue we have had to deal with recently is the phone. Philip really likes his iPhone. He likes to take notes on it; he likes to research information on it; he likes scrolling through Twitter and Instagram on it. I like all those things too, just not to the extent that he does. There have been times when I have felt that he is so focused with what is going on with all his social media friends that he is not engaging with me.

This is a real issue. What I want to do in these moments is get angry or pout (I probably have). This is not the mature conflict-resolution kind of girl I want to be, so instead I have learned to say something like, "I feel ignored or left out when you are on your phone while we are at dinner. Could this dinner be a phone-free one?" I want him to enjoy his phone and all the fun things on it. It is fun keeping up with our friends around the world! But I also want us to have times when we are enjoying each other.

Seek Good Counsel

Often in the middle of a disagreement or conflict with our spouse, we talk to others about it. That can be a good thing—but it depends on whom you are talking to.

I knew a woman who was having some serious marriage issues (we all do from time to time). I found out that she was spending quite a bit of her time with a group of girlfriends who had either been divorced a few times, were angry at men or were determined never to get married. What advice could this particular group of women give her that would be helpful? They told this woman things like, "Just leave him. You are smarter and more capable than he is." These weren't bad women; they were just not able to give her any tools for navigating the particular challenge she was in. They could not help her stay married in the face of the challenge she and her spouse were facing.

Get help when you need it, but make sure you are getting help from people who are further up the road than you are. If you want to build a successful business, get advice from someone who has done the kind of work you want to do. If you want to play an instrument, get lessons from someone who can play the same one. If you want to build a marriage, get input from people who are doing it well—happily married people who have the kind of relationship you would like to have.

Think Straight

Sometimes in the middle of conflict, I have to remind myself of Philip's good qualities. It is easy to get distracted by the annoying things—the annoying things are annoying. So many times the annoying things scream louder than the good qualities, so we have to intentionally concentrate on the good on purpose.

Just recently I was *so* irritated with Philip. Nothing major—just everything he did or didn't do bothered me. That triggered lots of thoughts, mostly about his weaknesses. I found myself dwelling on his weaknesses. Not good.

I spend time every day reading the Bible and praying, and one day I felt as if God said to me, "Holly, stop it. Take those thoughts captive. They are not producing anything good. Think on some things that are great about Philip." Well, it took some time. I wasn't so willing to quit my mental Philip bashing. But I did. It took me a minute to think of one thing I liked about him. One thing. That was all I could come up with for a while. Then one more.

Paul challenged the Philippians to look for the best in each other, and when we do that too, then God will work into us "his most excellent harmony."

> Summing it all up, friends, I'd say you'll do best by filling your minds and meditating on things true, noble, reputable, authentic, compelling, gracious—*the best, not the worst; the beautiful, not the ugly; things to praise, not things to curse*. Put into practice what you learned from me, what you heard and saw and realized. Do that, and God, who makes everything work together, will work you into *his most excellent harmonies* (Phil. 4:8-9, *THE MESSAGE*, emphasis added).

Conflict resolution.

Nobody said it would be easy.

And countless marriages fail because neither spouse wants to learn how to resolve the conflicts. If you leave your marriage thinking that the problem was just him or just her, I would like to suggest that you will have conflicts in your next marriage too.

Because two becoming one is not always a smooth process, you might as well learn some of the tools now. In the corporate and legal worlds, people are paid a lot of money to help resolve conflicts. You won't get the big bucks for resolving conflicts in marriage, but you will have the opportunity to build a lifelong partnership that is strong and lasting.

There are right and wrong ways to face and resolve conflict.

Fighting to the death verbally or physically is not the way. Total domination or complete submission should not be our only options in resolving conflict. Nor is holding and repressing tension or frustration until a massive blowout occurs a good way to handle our disagreements.

We must be willing to fight fair, to work toward compromise and to take divorce off the table. If divorce is not an option, we will work together toward solutions.

Crises will come. Remember that *we* is most important.

Weathering the Storms

Some conflicts arise in a marriage because of storms on the outside. Pervasive attitudes in our culture are one example. I actually believe that the pressure on our marriages today is much more severe than it was for our parents. The media certainly isn't helping either. How many happy (and not dysfunctional!) two-parent families do you see portrayed on television?

Humanism

The desire to put *me* first is a prevalent theme in our society today. Philip and I live in Hollywood, and this attitude permeates our city. We can't be foolish and think that this outlook won't affect us. Plenty of marriages end because one or both spouses have succumbed to the humanistic thought pattern, *I will do whatever is good for me, regardless of what my desires do to our marriage.* We might not say that out loud—it might be underneath our actions. This is the if-it-feels-good-do-it mentality, and it will destroy a marriage. *We* always has to be more important than *me* if a marriage is going to weather the storms of life.

Materialism

The quest for more and more stuff is another external pressure that can damage a marriage. We become so focused on working hard in order to gather things that we end up having less time to spend together. The media, in a not-so-subtle way, convinces us that the more stuff we have, the happier we'll be.

"This house isn't big enough; we need a bigger one."

"This car isn't new; we need a new one."

"My clothes are soooo last season; I need more."

Now I am not saying that we can't have a nice home, a new car or stylish clothes. I am saying that we should look at the cost. If we have to work three jobs or a job that requires 80 hours a week in order to pay for all the newer and better stuff, connecting with our spouse will be hard. And if we *can* make time for connection after that 80-hour workweek, chances are high that one or the other of us will be too exhausted or irritated to enjoy one another.

Materialism says, "Stuff is more important than relationships." Again, most of us would say that we don't believe that, but how are we living? Many times what we say we believe does not line up with our actions. J. Paul Getty was the wealthiest man in the world during his lifetime. He said, "I would give my entire fortune for one happy marriage." If you spend more time maintaining your lifestyle than maintaining your marriage, then the lack of intimacy and connection may cost you the relationship.

The Importance of Resiliency

Other storms can attack a marriage. These are the crises that come upon most of us at one time or another. We will all face a crisis that we did not anticipate, that we feel unprepared for. All of us will either lose a job, go bankrupt, be dragged into a lawsuit, live through a natural disaster, experience the death of a parent or a child, undergo the loss of friends, become disabled, contract a life-threatening disease . . . and the list goes on. When the worst happens, marriages whose foundations are already shaky and uncertain often crumble under the pressure.

After 9/11 our initial instinct as a nation and as families was to draw closer together. But when the initial shock wore off, some marriages were unable to survive. Delayed trauma and feelings of despair can shift our world. This was especially true for those who were directly affected by the tragedy or were involved in the rescue operations. Years later we have seen a sharp rise in divorce among firefighters and police officers whose lives were forever altered by the loss of colleagues, family members and friends.

In weathering the storms that come against a marriage, we need to be resilient people. We can't be so frail or so rigid that storms can destroy us.

Palm trees are so resilient that in a storm they will not break but instead bend to the earth. After the storm, they rise to their former state and continue their growth.

Buildings in Southern California, where I live, are built to withstand a great shaking. From new houses to the tallest Los Angeles skyscrapers, architects and builders have incorporated various designs and materials to help the buildings stand strong through earthquakes. Outside forces necessitate that offices and dwellings be built with resiliency.

And the building begins with a strong foundation.

Think about a general contractor. When he constructs a massive building, he doesn't start building on the asphalt or on the grass. He has to dig out the ground and make a solid foundation. Jesus tells us to build our house (our life) on the rock, which is Him, so that when storms come, the wind and the weather may beat on the house but will not be able to take it down (see Matt. 7:24-27). If we build our house on asphalt or grass or sand, as Jesus says, it won't take much stormy weather to completely destroy it.

Build well.

Some people appear to have a special capacity for optimism and resilience, while others are easily driven to despair when the balance of their lives is upset. Resilient people survive and even thrive in the face of struggle. Resilient couples are more likely to weather the large and small storms of life than those couples who are fearful and unsteady.[2]

In order to keep together through a crisis, remember that *we* is very important. Together *we* are stronger. Together *we* can get through this.

Don't isolate. You need each other. Don't blame. Blame separates.

It was not Philip's fault that I got cancer. It was not my fault. It just happened. Our marriage is different today because we had to navigate this crisis. We didn't handle it perfectly; we just handled it together. There were times when I made so many diet and health changes in one day that Philip's head was spinning—and he felt just a bit frustrated. There were times when he was not as conscious of what I was feeling as I would have liked. Regardless, we got through it together. There were some messy moments, but we are stronger today.

(By the way, I am eight years cancer free. YAY!)

Keeping a sense of humor is crucial for dealing with the crises that come. After the devastation of the 1994 earthquake in Los Angeles that caused severe damage in our home (our house cracked rather than swayed!), I remember Philip looking at the piles of shattered china on our kitchen floor and commenting, "Well, you said you wanted new dishes. Now I believe you!" We laughed for a moment and then began the long process of cleaning up. And we didn't stay at the cleanup process all day either. We took our kids, drove to a hotel in another county (one where the earth wasn't moving!) and got in a Jacuzzi. We took a few moments amid the crisis to make some fun. It helped.

Don't let the crisis separate you. Don't let the plans of the enemy bring division. Work through the crisis together.

Two are better than one, because they have a good return for their labor: If either of them falls down, one can help the other up. But pity anyone who falls and has no one to help them up! Also, if two lie down together, they will keep warm. But how can one keep warm alone? Though one may be overpowered, two can defend themselves. A cord of three strands is not quickly broken (Eccles. 4:9-12).

Seasons Change

Every marriage goes through different seasons. Some are more fun than others! Each season comes with its own rewards and challenges.

In the beginning of a marriage, while it is certainly still "the honeymoon," there is an adjustment needed as we each learn that we can't do what we want to do when we want to do it. There are now two of us. Someone else to consider. No longer a season of singleness but togetherness. New season.

Many of us have or will have children. Wow, they change our world, don't they? When our son, Jordan, was born, Philip and I were of course thrilled. Our baby was loved and welcomed. I just don't think we were prepared for the time, energy and stuff that come with having a baby. Is anyone? Living on little sleep and often not having much time together took its toll on our marriage. We had to work through that season. Then a few years later, along came our daughter. Even more juggling. Trying to find time for just Philip and I became very difficult, so again we had to make the time. We scheduled dates. If our marriage was going to make it through the baby and toddler phases, we were going to have to find time to spend together—as Philip and Holly, not just Daddy and Mommy.

Then there are seasons when our job might require lots of our time. That's great, as long as we are communicating with our spouse about it. About 18 years ago, I began to travel around the world speaking. This was a new season for us. At the beginning, it was a bit messy. I scheduled too many trips back to back with not enough breathing room in the middle. The traveling was fine—we both believed it was what God had for me—but we needed to schedule it so that it would work with our family and my responsibilities at our home church, The Oasis. No problem—just a new season that had to be navigated. It would have become a problem if we weren't talking about it and figuring it out together.

Many of us have had or will have teenagers in our homes. Exciting time of life, isn't it? I love that my children are becoming my friends. It is so encouraging to watch them walk out their own relationships with Jesus and discover what God put them on the planet to fulfill.

It is a great season, but it comes with its own challenges. Teens stay up late, so when our kids were teens, it was a bit tricky for Philip and me to find time for our own intimacy. I had to get over being embarrassed that they knew what was going on behind the closed door. When they were little, they had gone to bed before us, so it hadn't been an issue. Just another season of life! As teenagers, our kids were given more responsibility, including the privilege of having a car. That certainly helped with the errands—but at the same time, it made us pray more! And navigating the emotions of teenage girls can be tricky. I actually think I handled it more easily than Philip did, but it has taken both of us encouraging each other along the way to get through this season. Remember, you are on the same team!

What about the empty-nest season? This is where we are now. And I am loving it! I love the time with my adult children, and I love the time Philip and I get together. In many ways we have done the work over the last 29 years of building a marriage, so we still like each other (most days!)

I am not sure Philip and I will ever retire (not sure how to retire from building God's kingdom!), but I imagine that our daily work life will change. That will be a new season to look forward to and to negotiate.

And how about the grandparent season?

The great-grandparent season?

Determining to handle the seasons of life together will make all the difference in getting through them. You and your spouse are in this together, for the long haul!

And when you think about it, in spite of the conflicts, two really are better than one. In so many ways—from handling serious situations to dealing with everyday mundane things.

When ordering at a restaurant, you can share two dinners. You get the salad, and he orders the barbecue chicken. Perfect. Now he can have some salad, and you get some chicken. Two are better than one.

When at the grocery store, one of you can get in the long line while the other races to get the last two items. Two are better than one.

When entering the lodge after a long day of snow skiing, he can order your hot drink while you are still trying to get your skis off. Two are better than one.

When attempting to zip up a dress that might require you to dislocate your shoulder, he walks up and does it effortlessly. Two are better than one.

Talk—Listen—Talk—Listen

Deficient or failed communication is often listed as a reason for divorce. I actually think that lack of communication is *the* number-one reason for a broken marriage. Even if a couple says that their divorce was due to disagreements about finances or irreconcilable differences or even infidelity, I believe that any area of challenge could be overcome by better communication. If a couple has trouble with their finances and it produces stress, but they are great at talking about it, communicating will go a long way toward resolving their issue.

Communication is key.

The word "communication" is related to the Latin word *communis*, which means "to make common." Basically, communication is *making common* the needs, desires, thoughts and feelings of our hearts so that both parties can understand each other.

Communication is more than verbal. Our expressions, our body language, the look in our eyes and in our tone often have as much impact—sometimes more—than our words do. If you say "I love you" while looking into the eyes of your spouse in a gentle tone with a soft touch, the words are more believable than if you say them begrudgingly and looking away.

Same words. Different body language.

When it comes to communication, it all matters.

Saying "I'm sorry" is important in a marriage. Saying it sincerely and looking at your spouse when you do communicates the apology you want. Saying it reluctantly while looking down does not come across as a sincere apology. We often trust the accuracy of non-verbal behaviors more than the words themselves. Again, the content may be good, but the context in which the words are said is equally important.

Communication is the exchange and flow of information and ideas from one person to another. It involves a sender transmitting an idea, a thought or some information to a receiver. Effective communication occurs *only* if the receiver understands exactly the information or idea that the sender intended to transmit. Therein lies the problem. We think that just because we have said something we have communicated it, but as Freeman Teague Jr. once said, "Nothing is so simple that it cannot be misunderstood."

Often we don't communicate what we want to say; we might think we know what we are saying, but what we think we are saying is not what comes across.

Philip is a fan of the Beatles. When we were planning our annual GodChicks conference, he mentioned to me that he thought we should do one of their songs.

"Great idea," I said. "I'll find one that will fit."

"I have an idea for one," he said. When I asked him which one, he mentioned the song "Something." We listened to the song, and at first it seemed awesome. But then, right after the man in the song communicated his love and admiration for the woman, he made a comment about not being sure whether their love would grow or not.

Uhhh—this is not good. At least, it is not good if you are trying to communicate commitment and a forever love! We decided not to use that song because it did not say what we wanted to communicate.

The apostle Paul wrote to the church in Corinth about another difficult aspect of communication:

Oh, dear Corinthian friends! We have spoken honestly with you, and our hearts are open to you. There is no lack of love on our part, but you have withheld your love from us. I am asking you to respond as if you were my own children. Open your hearts to us! (2 Cor. 6:11-13, *NLT*).

In his letter Paul is saying that he has spoken honestly and freely to the Corinthian believers. His heart has been open, yet they have not reciprocated. He has been willing to communicate, but they have not.

In becoming better at communication in our marriages, we need to be willing. Be someone who is willing to open up. Be someone who will attempt to express the thoughts of your heart.

Philip will never know me, and we will never experience real intimacy, if I do not share with him the feelings, thoughts and ideas in my heart. The trick for me is being clear in what I am expressing. Am I saying what I think I am saying?

On the flip side, am I also creating an atmosphere in which Philip feels safe to open up to me? I cannot force him to open up, but I can do my part to create an atmosphere that makes it easy for him. Asking him for advice is one way to get him to open up: "What do you think about this situation?" Even if I think I know all the answers (I never do), I still ask what he thinks. The goal is to create an open atmosphere, not to prove someone right or wrong.

Another way I have found to help Philip open up is to express an interest in something he is interested in.

As I mentioned, Philip is a serious Yankees fan. Just ask how much Yankees stuff he has.

T-shirts.

Jerseys.

Coats.

Jackets.

Caps.

Watches.

Pictures.

Snow globes.

Beanies.

No kidding. He has the MLB application on his iPhone just so he can keep up with the Yankees games. He can be anywhere, turn on the app and watch those Yankees. Yippee. We manage to make it to New York City a few times each year, and interestingly enough, it is always during baseball season. Because I love my husband, I have become a Yankees fan (although I manage to be a fan without all the paraphernalia or the iPhone app).

If Philip has had a bad day or is frustrated with different issues and seems to be a little closed off, I can get him to open up if I start talking about baseball. If I start asking questions about Derek Jeter or about who is on the mound that day or about how many games ahead of the Boston Red Sox the Yankees are, within 10 minutes my husband is a different person.

Philip does the same for me. Occasionally I tell him the long version of what I am thinking, but mainly I stick to the streamlined version so that I can finish before his eyes start to glaze over.

Philip's parents were divorced when he was quite young. It was not a quiet, amicable divorce (I'm not sure how many of those there are). His parents fought, yelled, blamed each other and were so loud that the police were called. In fact, the police came to their house so many times that Philip knew the officers by name. As a child, he experienced communication at its worst. Nobody was honoring, nobody was listening, no one was creating a safe place for the family.

Philip's personality, as I mentioned before, is fairly introverted. He is someone who processes things within. Because of his background and his quiet personality, he has every excuse to be a poor communicator. And yet when we were dating, he was the one asking questions. He would ask me things like, "What do you think your strengths are?" "What are three things you wish I would talk to you about?" "What do you think my strengths are?"

He was creating an atmosphere in which feelings and thoughts could be expressed. Based on how he grew up, this tendency doesn't seem as if it would come naturally, yet Philip's desire was to head the opposite direction from where he'd come. He wanted to become an effective communicator.

Just last night as he and I were out to dinner, we asked each other lots of questions. Each of our five favorite movies, five favorite Bible verses, five favorite places we have visited. It was such a fun conversation. Lots of talking and listening. And just to be clear, we don't have these conversations all day every day—Philip would run out of words! We just chat like this every now and then in our effort to stay connected.

Perhaps just as important as expressing our thoughts clearly and creating an atmosphere for open communication is listening.

Now *hearing* and *listening* are not the same thing. Hearing is the act of perceiving sound. It simply refers to the reception of aural stimuli, which is involuntary. Listening, on the other hand, is a selective activity that involves the reception and the interpretation of aural stimuli. It involves decoding the sound into meaning.

Listening is divided into two main categories: passive and active. Passive listening is little more than hearing. It occurs when the receiver of the message has little motivation to listen carefully, such as when listening to music, storytelling and television or when being polite.

People generally speak at 100 to 175 words per minute (according to the people in my world, I speak about twice that fast!), but they can listen intelligently at 600 to 800 WPM. Because only a part of our mind has to pay attention to so few words, it is easy for us to go into "mind drift"—to think about other things while listening to someone. The cure for this is active listening, which involves listening with a purpose. It requires that the listener attend to the words and feelings of the sender in order to gain understanding. It takes the same amount of energy as, or even more than, speaking does.

It requires the receiver to hear the various messages, understand
the meaning and then verify the meaning by offering feedback.[3]

If we are going to be great at communicating in our marriages—
if we are going to be great at resolving conflict—we must become
active listeners. The apostle James offers us the recipe for great active
listening: "Everyone should be quick to listen, slow to speak and
slow to become angry" (Jas. 1:19). Active listeners spend more time
listening than talking. (I fail at this sometimes.) Active listeners do
not just appear to listen while actually waiting for a break in the
conversation to say what they want to say. (I fail at this sometimes
too.) Active listeners maintain eye contact, make encouraging noises
that let the talker know that he or she is being heard—noises like
"Hmmm," "Really," "Wow"—and they often take notes.

I have learned the benefits of note taking. Once Philip decides
to share something, he does not like to be interrupted with questions. I like it when he interrupts me with questions, because it lets
me know that he is listening—but that is just another way in which
men and women are different! Philip does not like interruptions,
because they make him forget where he was in the conversation.
So I write down my thoughts or questions and express them after
he is done sharing his thoughts.

Effective communication is a learned skill, and in each marriage
the dynamics might be different. We can all get better at opening
up, at talking and at really listening. And we must. If our marriages are going to make it through the conflicts that inevitably arise
from inside and outside, we must become stronger communica-
tors. Neither your past nor your personality should be an excuse
for poor communication.

Think It Through

Women

1. Peace with God opens the door for deeper relationship with Him; that deeper relationship allows us to talk with Him about our conflicts before speaking to our husband about them. Have you ever asked God to show you your part in a conflict? How did that change your perception and ultimate action?
2. What does timing have to do with resolving an issue? (Think about Esther.) How has poor timing affected your relationship? How did things go when you got the timing just right?
3. How about the place you choose to talk about an issue— why is that important? What is a good place for you and your husband to work through a problem?
4. "This is not about *his* problem or *my* problem. We are married. This is *our* problem." When conflicts arise, do you find yourself leaning toward *his*, *my* or *our*? How can you get better at staying on the same team with your husband?
5. Communication, both listening and speaking, is key. How do words, tone and body language work together in communication?

Men

1. Conflicts in marriage *will* arise (we're not clones, remember?). Hateful words, indifference and neglect can hurt your wife deeply. But how do they also hurt you?
2. How can being at peace with God help you in resolving conflict with your wife? Do you feel at peace with Him? Why or why not?
3. Do you find yourself saying, "I'm sorry, but …"? How can you determine to get great at saying, "I'm sorry" with no buts?
4. How we handle conflict is vitally important. Are you able to watch your mouth, or do you tend to say whatever

you are thinking whenever you think it? How can you do better?

5. Determining to handle the seasons of life together will make all the difference in getting through them. Think about past seasons with your wife (dating, getting married, having children, starting new jobs, moving and so on). How did these affect your marriage? Are you intentional about spending time with your wife and building intimacy in every season of life?

8

The Big Three: Faith, Finance and Forgiveness

Philip

The purpose of my instruction is that all believers
would be filled with love that comes from a pure heart,
a clear conscience, and genuine faith.
1 Timothy 1:5, *NLT*

And in the end, the love you take is equal
to the love you make.
The Beatles

In my opinion there are three things that can make or break a marriage. These three things lead to thousands of relationship breakdowns. I have had so many conversations with couples whose marriages were crumbling, and with a few questions, I have discovered that their root problems can be found in one of these areas.

Even though Holly and I have a great marriage, we also have to admit that we have a "high maintenance" marriage. Another way of saying this is that I am a high-maintenance kind of guy, and Holly can also be high maintenance. (In case Holly is reading this, I'd like to clarify that she is beautiful, talented, brilliant and a *bit* high maintenance.)

I have ADD. I lose things, I can't stay focused for real long, I go from project to project in a matter of seconds, and I forget things, like important people's names and things I was "supposed" to do. I say that this makes me interesting. I'm also a little OCD. Not a lot. A little. How do I describe this just the right way? I'm not so OCD that it brings everything to a stop, but I'm enough to make me frustrated when others don't notice what's wrong with certain details. Of course, I'm exaggerating these things a little bit for educational purposes.

I also worry about things; things that matter and things that don't really matter. I worry about my kids, our church—Oasis Church—the weather, the Dodgers, what people will think and, in direct violation of the teachings of Jesus, I worry about tomorrow.

Holly, on the other hand, is energetic, unreasonably optimistic and kind of a germaphobe. She likes to do things quickly and now. Right now! "Go!" She probably has the metabolism of the average bumblebee. She's already told you that her style of project management can be ready, fire, aim. Imagine the joy this brings to my OCD moments. She is an extremely positive person. That's good, right? But where is the line between positive and overly optimistic? She can be so positive that I wonder if she has a bit of reality deficiency.

We went through an earthquake that brought $60,000 worth of damage to our home, including all our dishes being smashed to pieces. Holly said, "Well, I wanted to get new dishes anyway!"

I too am an optimist, but I'm an optimist who takes his raincoat.

You see, normal human beings can appear to be depressed when around my wife. World-class cheerleaders can seem despondent when Holly's around.

Well, anyway—what was I talking about?

Oh yeah, we have a high-maintenance marriage. It might help you and your spouse to just admit your little idiosyncrasies. If you are normal, you have issues, and your issues can bring tension into your relationship. Most people probably have high-maintenance relationships. If you don't agree with this, just go with me here, because it makes me feel better about my relationship. We have found that these "big three" are crucial for us in keeping our marriage in its happy place.

The First of the Big Three: Faith

I'm not talking about a chosen religion, even though religion can have a huge impact on relationships. I'm talking about a real and genuine faith that brings the actual presence of God into our everyday, real-life circumstances. It is a living and active faith.

Marriage is not made for just two people. It's made for three. It works best with a man, a woman and God. Does that sound like a cheesy cliché to you? I'm not sure how else to say it, but I'll try. Marriage works when God is present in it, guiding and impacting our relationship.

When we think of relationships, dating and marriage, most people don't think that God or faith is a big factor. But we need God to help us love like we want to love. We need to express a love that goes deeper than what we can do.

There is a crucial balance between our own relationship-savvy efforts and our faith in God to bring His touch to our home. I don't believe that God solves all problems without any effort on our part, and I also don't think that all problems are spiritual in nature.

I may or may not have prayed, "Lord if you could just change Holly, our marriage would really be great." And Holly, I'm sure, has thought, *Is the devil attacking our marriage, or is my husband just clueless?*

Maybe a little of both.

But seriously, prayer by either spouse individually or together can help dramatically. Couples who regularly make prayer an essential part of their life have a higher rate of marital success. Getting direction for our life from the Bible can be so powerful, especially in the middle of life battles that we are facing. We can also see that some humility and respect are necessary in our heart to make our relationship more intimate. When we add to those a genuine admiration of our spouse, we can reach new levels of happiness.

I can't overemphasize the fact that regular and consistent involvement in a lively, active local church can make all the difference in a marriage.

James tells us that faith and the right works are necessary:

Faith by itself isn't enough. Unless it produces good deeds, it is dead and useless. Now someone may argue, "Some people have faith; others have good deeds." But I say, "How can you show me your faith if you don't have good deeds? I will show you my faith by my good deeds" (Jas. 2:17-18, *NLT*).

Without faith, God's help and the relationship wisdom God provided, Holly's and my marriage would not have survived.

It's important to do the powerful and practical things that have a real impact in marriage (like the stuff you are reading about in this book—just sayin'), but we cannot neglect the undeniable spiritual component. Faith. The amazing thing is, God is asking to be invited into our marriage. "Look! I stand at the door and knock. If you hear my voice and open the door, I will come in, and we will share a meal together as friends" (Rev. 3:20, *NLT*).

Every one of us has needs that no human can meet.

All of us. Even you.

We have many problems in relationships because we try to get from *people* what we can only get through a real faith in God. We also have problems in relationships because we don't know how to activate this faith. We don't know how to love like God loves. Jesus is known for His compassion and His love for all people. We need that kind of love in our life.

Marriage without an active engagement with God is a problem waiting to happen. Let's look at some of the common needs of both men and women that must be met mainly by God Himself.

Acceptance

God accepts us just as we are. Some people's religion or their view of what religions teach could be very different. In the New Testament we learn that God has extended His love to us unconditionally. This kind of love is incredibly attractive to us, but it's impossible for us to conjure up on our own.

On my worst day, I want someone to love me despite how I act. Mostly, people love us because of *what they don't know* about us. We have a deep fear that if people really knew us, our thoughts, our past mistakes and the awful things we may have participated in, they would no longer love us.

I heard author Tony Campolo once say to an audience, "If you knew everything about me, you would not be here listening to me. But don't get so self-righteous; if I knew everything about you, I wouldn't be talking to you."

In the frailty of our humanity, we say to others, "Judge not." And then we judge them for violating our understanding of this comment.

Identity

Who are we, anyway? Most of us get our identity from a variety of places: our accomplishments, our experiences, our failures, the accusations made against us or the inner voices that holler at us. The biggest danger in life is getting our identity from what others say about us. Good or bad.

We find our identity in our relationships, family or friends. If that goes sour, then our identity is shattered, and so is our sense of self. We are tempted to think, "If my husband [wife, dad, girlfriend, co-worker, etc.] doesn't love me, then maybe I'm not loveable."

If people say good things about us, but we don't really believe the things they say, we need to hear those words of affirmation daily, or we will tend to descend toward our fear that we aren't that valuable after all. Those closest to us may say, "He seems so needy. He's always sucks the life out of me, because he's always looking for reassurance."

We can get our identity from God. He loves us. We are His chosen and loved sons and daughters. God has invested the highest possible amount in our life. If the value of something is based on the price paid for it, then you and I are valuable beyond measure. In a fully invested faith in God, we can begin to see ourselves the way God speaks of us in His Word. We are His chosen ambassadors of compassion, faith and peace. Holly wrote lots of good stuff about this in chapter 1.

Security

What do you do to satisfy your need for security?

Here's how to figure out where you place your security: think of the things that you worry about the most. That's probably where your sense of security lies. If we worry about money or provisions, about having a great reputation or a hot-looking wife, then we feel insecure. If we have enough of those things, we feel safe.

The prophet Isaiah challenged the Israelites, "Why do you spend money for what does not satisfy?" (see Isa. 55:2). Great question. Why put our greatest resources into what will never satisfy us in the first place?

If we don't get our needs met by God, we automatically turn to people and things to fulfill those needs. It will completely transform our life when we get our security from our faith in God and His Word.

Jesus says to us, "Come to me, all of you who are weary and carry heavy burdens, and I will give you rest" (Matt. 11:28, *NLT*).

The Second of the Big Three: Finances

People's financial worlds are complicated. They involve our upbringing, worldview, fears, experiences, dreams and self-imposed limitations. I like what Will Smith is quoted as saying, "Too many people spend money they haven't earned to buy things they don't want to impress people they don't like."

There are a few areas in our lives that we don't like people to stick their nose into. Among those areas are sex, how we raise our children and our finances. "Hey, that's personal. It's none of your business." That may be true, but these are also areas in which most people need a lot of help.

Couples can be tremendously frustrated sexually and yet resist help from those who actually have some answers. Children can throw daily tantrums in public or look their parents in the eye and do exactly the opposite of what has been asked of them, but often parents don't want any help in raising that sweet little critter who is already in charge of the home and family. "She's just a little tired today—that's why she threw a bottle at you, Pastor Philip."

More couples fight over finances than over anything else. Relationships fall apart and marriages blow up over this one issue. It's important for a couple to come up with a financial strategy, to agree on it and to follow it as soon as possible.

I have a few recommendations below for the financial area of marriage.

Get Professional Guidance

This can be through a book like *Financial Makeover* by Dave Ramsey or from others like it. This can also be accomplished in pre-marital counseling while preparing for marriage.

This is called creating a budget. When we don't have a budget, we tend to make emotional decisions with our money. With a budget we make better decisions and less emotionally inspired decisions. It helps us to agree on values and plans. A budget provides accountability and measures the effectiveness of how we are earning and spending.

Make sure that savings is a priority in your plan. Saving is one of the most important financial skills you can develop.

Remember, living with a budget is not legalistically following a plan but adhering to a guideline that will help you finance your dreams.

Holly was raised in a family that was financially secure, and I was raised in a family that had very little. When we first got married, I told Holly that we needed to start living on a budget. She cried. She thought that this meant we were poor. See what I'm dealing with here? As if the car I was driving wasn't enough of a sign.

"No," I explained to her. "We do not need to live on a budget because we are poor. We need to live on a budget so we won't become poor." All her life Holly had been able to ask her mother and dad for something, and they would give it to her. She quickly found out that I was not her dad.

I have to say here that many times Holly's parents' generosity to us has provided much help for us over the years.

Honor God with Your Financial Decisions

Ask God for financial wisdom and direction, and be willing to follow it. I didn't say ask God for help. I said wisdom. Pray about and get wisdom for all major financial decisions.

Honoring God includes dedicating your finances to God and asking Him for direction. Our plans need to honor God, our values need to honor God, and our actions need to honor God.

King Solomon was the richest man who ever lived in the Bible. He tells us,

> By wisdom a house is built, and through understanding it is established; through knowledge its rooms are filled with rare and beautiful treasures (Prov. 24:3-4).

I want the wisdom of God in our home. I want the knowledge that I could only get through God's direction to us. Everybody needs to have a good plan in how he or she will . . .

Earn money
Spend money
Save money
Give money

It's important to you and it's important to God that you get this right. One in 25 verses in the New Testament addresses the stewardship of our possessions. There are over 2,000 Scriptures in the Bible about money, possessions and wealth. Here's one: "Honor the LORD with your wealth, with the firstfruits of all your crops; then your barns will be filled to overflowing, and your vats will brim over with new wine" (Prov. 3:9-10).

Honoring God includes finding contentment in what we have now. Jesus tells us about a paradox in life: the more we have, the less happy and peaceful we are. The lack of contentment can rob us of so much, including faith, joy, peace, love and blessing. We need to discover how to be content with what we have now and to trust God to lead and provide for the future.

We may need to downsize a little to begin to get our financial world in order. It's better to be in a small house and to be happy than to be in a big house and to be broke or in debt.

> Don't store up treasures here on earth, where moths eat them and rust destroys them, and where thieves break in and steal. Store your treasures in heaven, where moths and rust cannot destroy, and thieves do not break in and steal. Wherever your treasure is, there the desires of your heart will also be. . . . No one can serve two masters. For you will hate one and love the other; you will be devoted to one and despise the other. You cannot serve both God and money. . . . So don't worry about these things, saying, "What will we eat? What will we drink? What will we wear?" These things dominate the thoughts of unbelievers, but your heavenly Father already knows all your needs. Seek the Kingdom of God above all else, and live righteously, and he will give you everything you need (Matt. 6:19-21,24,31-33, *NLT*).

Honoring God includes discovering the secret of God's blessing. The Bible teaches us about a timeless principle that will lead to God's blessing and provision in our life. It was practiced both before the Law of Moses and in the New Testament, and it is still practiced in current times. It's called the tithe. Literally, "tithe" means "a tenth." The Holy Scriptures reveal that one tenth of what comes into our life through income, gifts and other sources are to be given to God through the local church. Read what Moses says is a command that came from God:

> One-tenth of the produce of the land, whether grain from the fields or fruit from the trees, belongs to the LORD and *must be set apart to him as holy* (Lev. 27:30, *NLT*, emphasis added).

You can mess with this "holy tenth" if you want to or disqualify it if you dare, but it will be at your own peril. I never could understand why people wouldn't want to be blessed by God.

Here is God's bold challenge and simple instruction to us that will unlock His provision in our life:

> "Bring all the tithes into the storehouse so there will be enough food in my Temple. If you do," says the LORD of Heaven's Armies, "I will open the windows of heaven for you. I will pour out a blessing so great you won't have enough room to take it in! Try it! Put me to the test!" (Mal. 3:10, *NLT*).

Holly and I have tithed for 30 years. We don't make this decision to tithe every week or every month—we made it once, 30 years ago, and we have never regretted anything that we've given to the local church.

It is dramatically clear that God desires you and me to be generous people, just as He is generous with us. After we have given God His holy portion of our income, then we can begin to be generous.

It would be wise to make this a priority in your financial plan.

Agree Before Acting Financially

It is vital that we include our spouse's ownership of our money and his or her financial perspective in our decisions. As a married couple, the money is *our* money. If you can't trust a person with that level of vulnerability, you should not be married yet.

Ideas like "It's my job that brought this money in, so I'm buying what I want" or "It's my aunt who died and left this inheritance, so I'm buying a car no matter what you say" can bring division and distrust. Inappropriate dominance or control can destroy the best of marriages.

Some men feel that it's their God-given right to control the money because of their title of "husband." Some women feel as if they should control the money because of their better math skills. No one should *control* the money. That will destroy a relationship. A couple should have a mutually created plan that they talk through and agree on. If you need to get help from a qualified third party, then do it. It is not a sign of weakness—it is a sign of integrity.

Resolve disagreements about financial decisions quickly. Don't use money as a weapon by spending it or controlling it. Don't keep secret bank accounts or "my money" that your spouse is not included in. This will build misunderstanding that can take a lot of work to overcome.

Avoid Unnecessary Debt as a Contagious Disease

If your financial plan is a good one, it will keep you out of debt or help you get out of debt. Make a commitment to no longer live the earn-a-thousand-dollars-and-spend-twelve-hundred plan. That plan is a debt trap. Make sure you have a good strategy to pay off debts and to live without debt unless a financial consultant advises an exception. Sometimes it is appropriate to borrow for things that will appreciate in value—a home or a business might be worth a great deal more later than when you made the investment in it. But even in the purchase of a home, you can get stuck with huge debts.

Following these simple ideas can radically change your relationship in regard to finances.

The Last of the Big Three: Forgiveness

If you married someone who is not normal—not like you—they are not weird, just different. And they will make mistakes. I have said things I wish I had never said; I have done things I'm embarrassed to reveal; and I've thought things that were destructive. I've needed forgiveness, and Holly has needed forgiveness. If you and your spouse are normal, you will both need forgiveness.

In the awesome description of love in 1 Corinthians 13, we read, "Love is patient, love is kind. It does not envy, it does not boast, it is not proud. It does not dishonor others, it is not self-seeking, it is not easily angered." Then these verses declare that love "keeps no record of wrongs. . . . Love never fails" (1 Cor. 13:4-5,8).

Love keeps no record of wrongs? If you are like me at all, you know that you need God's help with this one. Because we can be quick with coming up with a list of all her failures! In order for us to have the marriage we've always imagined was possible, we need to become champions at forgiveness.

We are challenged to this standard in the New Testament: "Be kind and compassionate to one another, forgiving each other, just as in Christ God forgave you" (Eph. 4:32).

There is a really high standard set here. A healthy and thriving marriage is made up of two people who know how to forgive one another. We have to be able to forgive the little things and the big things. Ladies, you need to forgive that fact that he leaves his socks on the floor and also be quick to forgive when he wounds you with a careless and cold statement. Guys, we have to forgive her when she disregards what we said and goes ahead as if we never expressed our thoughts, and we have to forgive her sarcastic, critical comment that embarrasses us in front of everyone.

This is not the kind of forgiveness that lets things go for now but is ready to bring out a list of mistakes when the next battle evolves. I hope you will discover the reality that forgiveness is the highest expression of love.

If we want to get our Black Belt in forgiveness, we need to be able to forgive for the petty frustrations that have been adding up, grievances that have never been resolved and the nagging that drives us crazy.

Tear up IOUs. Those lists. That score card.

If one of the biggest problems in relationships is unmet needs, then there will need to be a lot of forgiveness.

When Holly asks me for emotional support, I get logical. When grace would be the appropriate approach at a given moment, I get critical. She might think, *Can you be more stupid?* (Oh yeah, I'm not done yet. I've just started.) I apologize and then repeat my mistake a few weeks later.

More forgiveness required.

In the movie *Rain Man*, Dustin Hoffman plays an autistic genius who could instantly solve the most complicated math calculations and remember amazing details that appeared superhuman. He also kept a notebook, including random events that occurred during his day. He included offenses or perceived violations that his brother, Raymond, had committed. He wrote things like,

- 2:00 PM Raymond grabbed my arm and caused a lot of pain.
- Saturday morning, 9:00 AM. Raymond yelled at me and scared me.

It seemed ridiculous in the movie, but you might recognize that you probably do something similar:

- February 10. Holly interrupted me twice in three minutes, and then I forgot what I was saying.
- February 11. Holly interrupted me again, so it made me forgot what I was going to write down in this chapter.
- 3:00 PM. Philip did not respond the way I expected him to. Ughhh!

Ridiculous, right? Forgiveness is a gift you give yourself. Forgiveness is a gift you give your marriage.

> Do to others as you would have them do to you. If you love those who love you, what credit is that to you? Even sinners love those who love them (Luke 6:31-32).

Sometimes we let the unrealistic expectations we have of others ruin our love. Sometimes we cannot let go of a past offense. But we can't get where we want to go if we drive with our rearview mirror larger than our windshield. We have to learn how to get past our past.

Many of us may have to forgive major offenses of our spouse. It could be a moral failure, an addiction to some substance, a pornography obsession or even adultery. I'm not suggesting that you subject yourself to abuse, a serial adulterer, STDs or violence, but I am suggesting that divorce is not always the best solution. That maybe someone who has failed, been caught and is working hard to recover and regain trust should be given an opportunity to do so.

It is true that the Scriptures allow for divorce when a spouse has been unfaithful or left you behind, but that may not be the best solution in every situation. It's important to know that many great marriages have survived unfaithfulness and have found a deeper level of trust and intimacy than before the offense.

Christianity is the only religion that presents forgiveness as its core belief. Forgiveness, as I mentioned earlier, is the greatest expression of love.

I sat in a gathering of several thousand people and listened to Joyce Meyer tell of being sexually abused by her dad, many times, when she was a young girl. Her story continued with great detail of her journey of faith and forgiveness. At the end of her father's life, she had forgiven her dad, prayed with him for salvation and participated in baptizing him. That is an example of God's grace and forgiveness.

One of my favorite organizations in the world is Watoto Ministries in Kampala, Uganda. Their work in the city of Gulu has led them to reach women and children who were former child soldiers abducted by the LRA. I have heard the horrific stories of violations and tragedies imposed upon these beautiful people. They have been through unthinkable tragedies: they have been raped, forced to commit murder and to dismember others, have witnessed the rape of others and endured abuse after abuse.

Then we hear the end of their story that includes love and forgiveness, which is healing for them and mind-boggling to me.

Forgiveness for big offenses is difficult, disappointing and sometimes disillusioning. Rebuilding a marriage after it has been broken is like trying to piece together shattered glass.

If you are the offender in a relationship, don't act as if you deserve to be trusted. Trust is earned. Go ahead and start working on it.

There is healing; trust can be rebuilt. And couples who find their way through forgiveness often come away with a deeper, more intimate and more amazingly fulfilling relationship. It takes time, it takes work, it takes patience, and sometimes it may seem impossible, but it is worth the effort.

Keep short accounts. Are you holding offenses against your spouse? Don't let the sun go down on anger and resentment.

In the story *Les Misérables* (the one with Liam Neeson, Claire Danes and Geoffrey Rush—not the one with the singer Russell Crowe), the main character, Jean Valjean, is imprisoned for 19 years because he stole a loaf of bread.

When he gets out of prison, he is shown hospitality by a bishop. He tells the bishop of his desire to be a new man.

But in a moment of opportunity, the temptation is too great, and Valjean steals some silver and sneaks away into the night. Valjean is stopped by the police and asked where he got the silver utensils. He tells them that they were a gift from the bishop. The police don't buy his tale, and they tell him that he and they are going to go back to the bishop to check his story.

When they return to the monastery, Jean waits to hear the words that will return him to prison until he dies. But instead he hears the bishop say to the lawmen, "Of course this silver was my gift. But Jean Valjean, you took only part of it. You forgot the most valuable pieces. You forgot to take the silver candlesticks." And the bishop offers the other pieces of silver to Valjean. The police are convinced and leave Valjean to talk to the bishop.

The bishop afterward says to Valjean, "You must never forget this moment; never forget it. You've promised to be a new man; with this silver I've bought back your soul. Your soul and your life have been bought back. I've ransomed you from fear and hatred. You are not your own. From now on you belong to God."

The rest of Valjean's life was shaped and guided by this act of love and forgiveness.

This story reminds me of the statement Jesus made to the religious leaders of His day who were making accusations against a sinful woman. "I tell you, her many sins have been forgiven—as her great love has shown. But whoever has been forgiven little loves little" (Luke 7:47).

Remember the big three, and you will discover the truth that *love works.*

Think It Through

Women

1. Do you have a high-maintenance marriage? Do you think every marriage is high maintenance?
2. Without God as the third party in your marriage, you will be unable to purely love your husband. Think of those moments when it might feel hard for you to love your husband, and invite God into your marriage in that area. Are you open to watching what He will do? Reflect on how God has helped you love your husband through hard times.
3. Do you seek acceptance, identity and security from your husband or from God? What can you do to transfer any expectations you have on your husband to God?
4. How do finances affect your marriage? How can you and your husband work together on matters of budgeting, tithing and dealing with debt? How you can trust God with these concerns?
5. It's not always easy to forgive when you have been wronged. Remember the story of Jean Valjean and how forgiveness forever changed him? What can you do to get rid of IOUs and score cards and instead to forgive your husband when you feel wronged? Doing so could start a revolution in your marriage.

Men

1. "Marriage is not made for just two people. It's made for three." What do you think of this statement? Is God a part of your marriage? How would inviting Him to share in your marriage affect your relationship with your wife?
2. Do you and your wife do life in the context of a local church? Why is this so important?

3. Which aspect of financial stewardship is hardest for you: Being content with what you have, tithing, considering your money not "mine" but "ours" or staying out of debt? What is one practical step you can take to trust God with your finances?

4. Does forgiveness come easily for you, or is it difficult for you to forgive? What is something, big or small, that you can forgive your wife for today? Remember, forgiveness can help rebuild trust and revive a marriage!

9

Shift Happens

Holly

There is no more lovely, friendly,
and charming relationship, communion,
or company than a good marriage.
Martin Luther

Let marriage be held in honor (esteemed worthy, precious,
of great price, and especially dear) in all things.
Hebrews 13:4, *AMP*

A few years ago, Philip and I visited Seaside, Florida. Seaside has to be the most perfect-looking town I have ever seen. People in this master-planned community, both visitors and residents, rode bicycles along the perfectly groomed sidewalks to the perfectly clean Starbucks, to the perfectly decorated stores, to the perfectly designed school, to the perfectly adorable post office, to the perfectly refreshing ice-cream parlor, to the perfectly beautiful chapel, to the perfectly stocked grocery store, to the perfectly appointed restaurants, to the perfectly sandy beach—and then back to their perfectly designed homes or hotels.

As someone who comes from the city of Los Angeles—which is far from perfect looking—this was a new experience for me. Riding around on my bicycle in this perfect town, I felt as if I were on a movie set. In fact, I was. Seaside, Florida, is the community that was used in the filming of the movie *The Truman Show*. The movie is about a man who is unaware that he lives in a totally controlled environment. All the perfection around him—nice as it is—is a total fabrication.

Unlike Truman, we don't live in a bubble.

Our marriages must not only exist but also thrive in the real world, with all its distractions and complications. Most of us do not live out our marriage on some remote desert island where we get to focus entirely on our spouse for 24 hours a day. Nope. We have to work out our marriages with all the elements of life that come with being alive in the 21st century.

How do we do that and not lose sight of each other?

Here's Looking at You, Kids

Before I got married I had six theories about bringing up children; now I have six children and no theories. —John Wilmot, Earl of Rochester

Children are a heritage from the LORD, the fruit of the womb a reward (Ps. 127:3, *ESV*).

My children are a blessing. Most of the time. It has certainly been work raising them, and there have been moments along the way when I wondered how I would get through a particular parenting phase—or if *they* would survive it! The miracle of it all is looking at their faces and seeing some of me, some of Philip and mostly just them. They are wonderfully unique individuals with their own purpose in God.

For many of us, children are part of our life as we work out our marriage. We might want to ship them off to Siberia sometimes, but we don't. The real problem comes when our children become the center of our marriage.

From birth to 18 years old is 6,570 days. Obviously, our children remain our children forever, but our day-in, day-out input in their lives lasts about 6,570 days. In contrast, if Philip and I are blessed to have a 60-year marriage (just 35 more years to go!), we will have been married 21,900 days.

6,570 days.

21,900 days.

Do the math.

The time we have our children with us is much shorter than the span of our marriage, which is why it is not in the best interest of our marriage relationship to make our children the center. Our kids are a vital part but not the center.

I made this mistake with my son, Jordan. When he was born, I did not leave him, even for a few hours, for many months. He was the center of my world. His needs took priority over Philip's. His cry was louder and more demanding than my husband's request, so I accommodated my son. My marriage ended up on the back burner. It wasn't a conscious decision; it just happened as I looked to meet the needs of Jordan instead of my husband. Eventually, I started feeling more and more disconnected from Philip.

I had some ground to make up.

Fixing the out-of-whack dynamic was a two-step process. First, I had to get Jordan on some kind of schedule so that he fit in with our family instead of running it. (There are some great parenting resources out there that can help couples with this.) And second, I needed to go on a date with my husband. We needed some hours together as a couple. Jordan would be fine.

Over the years we have learned that regardless of the ages of our children, Philip and I need time as a couple. Time away from the kids. Time to remind each other that we got together for relationship, not just for the work of a family. If we don't take that time, our "communication" sounds like this:

"Who's cooking dinner?"

"Who's picking up the kids?"

"Did you sign the permission slip?"

"He forgot his lunch; can you take it to the school?"

All necessary communication, but intimacy requires just a bit more!

Do your homework to find a good babysitter, and go out to dinner. Go on a walk. Do something that helps you connect on a regular basis.

We have also made it a practice to have not only a family vacation but also a Philip-and-Holly vacation. When our children were younger, we would often just be gone a few nights and then come back to get the kids before embarking on our longer family vacation. But eventually, Philip and I would spend a week together somewhere, just the two of us, and then Paris and Jordan might join us. But that week alone with Philip would remind me why I married him! We needed that time away on our own.

I have talked to some couples with young children who say that they would love to go out, but their children cry when they leave, and that makes it too hard. I understand that. I remember how hard it was initially to leave our children in the hands of a babysitter, no matter how qualified he or she was. But let me tell you what Mom and Dad going out on a date teaches the children. It teaches them that the husband-wife relationship is a very high priority in the family. It teaches them that Mommy and Daddy love to spend time together. The best thing you can do for your children is to love each other.

We are to love our kids. We want the best for them. But making them the center of the family universe is not in their best interest. It also does not serve our world to have a generation of young people who think the world revolves around them. It will certainly not serve your marriage well either.

We also had to be careful about how many activities Jordan and Paris got involved in. I loved watching them both in various sports over the years, but I tried to limit their involvement to one sport at a time. Otherwise, Philip and I would be so busy keeping up with their schedules that it would be tricky for us, in our already full lives, to find time together.

As children become teenagers, life can get exciting. Just remember that you and your husband are one. Present a united front. Do not let your children or their desires drive a wedge between you. If you and your spouse disagree about the way something should be handled with your teenage children—driving, curfew, spending the night, whatever—don't disagree in front of them. Discuss the disagreement behind closed doors; in front of your children, present a united front.

Really, parenting is the procedure of teaching and training your children to leave your home and to begin lives of their own. Might sound strange, but it is true. Our job is to equip them to live well.

"That is why a man leaves his father and mother and is united to his wife, and they become one flesh" (Gen. 2:24). Children are supposed to leave, and parents are supposed to stay. Thus, your marriage should be at the top of the priority list. Navigating children is fun, but it is also work. Don't let the work of it cause you to lose sight of each other.

The People We Bring

The wise man must remember that while he is a descendant of the past, he is a parent of the future. —Herbert Spencer

Most of us have parents and in-laws as part of our lives. Some might be supportive and releasing, while others might be manipulative and try to control your marriage.

I have seen marriages seriously damaged because a couple did not know how to disconnect from controlling parents—and even from well-meaning parents who did not respect the new family. My goal is to be the releasing kind of parent and mother-in-law. I have some amazing girlfriends who have already walked this road; they are present in their adult children's lives to offer help if wanted, but they allow their children to live their own lives. I have watched them bite their tongues rather than offer unsolicited advice. Lord, help me to be the same!

We are to honor our parents. We are to respect and appreciate the position they hold in our lives. And yet we are to leave them. Once again, look at this direction from our God: "That is why a man *leaves his father and mother* and *is united to his wife*, and they become one flesh" (Gen. 2:24, emphasis added).

Your parents should not have more influence over you than your spouse does. In the beginning of my marriage, it was so tempting to call my mom and complain to her about Philip whenever he wasn't acting how I thought he should. *So* glad I didn't go there. I'm not sure why I didn't, because I certainly made plenty of other mistakes. I guess I just knew that while I was very grateful for the family that had raised me, I had left them to begin my own family. And to do that meant that I couldn't run to my mommy and

daddy whenever something did not go my way. Philip and I had to
work things out.

Your parents did the best they could to build their home. Now it
is your turn. Feel free to get advice from your mom or your dad. Take
the best of what they did and use it in your own home. Just remember that you are building your own family, and your parents' input
should never create division in your marriage.

As our parents become older, there will be changes. Who will
take care of them? Will they go to a retirement home? Will they live
with you? Choose whatever you feel is right; just make sure there is
dialogue about it between you and your husband. Recently my dad
has started to develop dementia. It has been so sad for me to watch
this man who was a high-powered executive and my personal biggest
cheerleader decline into someone who just sits there. My mom needs
help, and so we have decided that my parents will live with my sister
for a while. She has the room, so this is what will work right now.
We may reevaluate in a few years. I have been emotional through this
process and have really leaned on Philip and his strength to help me
navigate it. We have worked hard to stay united.

Along with our families, we bring our past into our marriage. Good
and bad. Each of us enters adulthood with a different background.
And that background has an effect on our marriage. Sometimes the
past feels like a third person invading our present.

My friend Priscilla Shirer was a guest speaker at our GodChicks
conference 2008. She told a great story that has stuck with me.

Priscilla and her husband, Jerry, went to minister at a local
church. When they arrived, a little exhausted from the weeks that
had led up to this visit, they were grateful to get some rest in their
hotel room. After settling in for the night, they were awakened in a
panic around eleven by the sound of a train barreling past their room,
whistle blaring. After their near-heart attack, they fell back asleep—
only to be jarred from sleep when the same sound paraded by at one
o'clock—and again at five thirty in the morning. So much for resting!

When a woman from the church arrived the next morning to
drive them to the meeting, Priscilla kindly mentioned that the loudest train on the entire planet kept them up through the entire night.
The girl's face turned white as a sheet when she realized what had
kept Priscilla and Jerry up all night. She apologized profusely and

said that the people like herself who had lived in the town for years could no longer hear the train.

I'd like to suggest that many of us are the same way. We are so used to the voices of our past whistling around in our minds that we don't even notice them anymore. We may have lived with depression, insecurity, jealousy, self-loathing, lust and pride for so long that we no longer recognize their daily impact on our lives.

But like Priscilla and Jerry in that little train-deaf town, a new person invited into our environment won't get much rest with all that disruption emanating from us. What is normal background noise to us can be annoying or even disturbing to our partner. Hidden issues come out of hiding. In light of another's perspective, we are forced to face our issues. Our spouse doesn't share our exact struggles, so what we have successfully and temporarily mastered will sound like a roaring train to him or her. The past becomes a third person, invading our marriage in the present.

Maybe we had parents who loved us and loved each other, so we are confident in relationships. There are others of us who have been hurt and betrayed and who aren't quite so secure in building relationships.

Maybe we come from years of abuse and are now on the healing journey (and it is a journey), and our spouse will have to be patient while we walk it out. There will be times when our past will interfere with our present. It might be frustrating, but both husband and wife have to remain focused on what they are building together.

Maybe he comes from a single-mother home and really had no idea what a husband—much less a father—should do. When she marries him, she is committing to encourage him on that journey and to work through the frustrations that come with it.

Maybe he expects a home-cooked meal every night because that's how his mom did it—and she has never even been in a kitchen. Maybe she expects him to fix whatever breaks around the house—and he has never even held a hammer. Our pasts, along with the expectations that come from them, *will* enter into the reality of our marriage. So be prepared to deal with them together.

Often our past will include a relationship or two. Philip was not the first person to ask me to marry him. He is the only one to whom I said, "I do."

Like most of us, I came into my marriage with a past. Not a sordid one, because the truth is, I only dated great guys. I never spent time with a man who did not treat me with respect and kindness. You know that saying that you have to kiss a lot of frogs before one becomes a prince? Not true—I wasted no time with frogs. Honestly, I only have great memories of the men I dated before I met Philip.

My memories of previous boyfriends are good ones—but that can be a problem too. In the first few years of our marriage, whenever I was mad about something Philip had done (or not done), my head filled with thoughts of a past boyfriend who, in that moment, I could only remember as being perfect. I would think, *I should have stayed with so and so; he wouldn't be treating me this way.* Not true. I had said no to that guy for a reason.

Our past, with its expectations and relationships, will have an influence on our marriage. It is crucial that we watch where our thoughts lead us. Stay focused on today. Stay engaged in this relationship that you are building.

What Friends Are For

How rare and wonderful is that flash of a moment when we realize we have discovered a friend. —William Rotsler

Friendship is always a sweet responsibility, never an opportunity. —Khalil Gibran

The friends we do life with have a crucial role to play in our marriage. They can either be a help and an encouragement or a drain and a detriment. The people we include in our world are so very important.

Most of us begin marriage with a list of his friends and a list of her friends.

This is good. Hopefully, you married someone who knows how to build friendships. And hopefully, most of his or her friends were supportive of your marriage. His friends and her friends, however, haven't ever known you as a married person. A married person now has another person to consider in every decision.

Before a couple is married, she might have been able to go to the movies with the girls without talking to anyone about it, or he might have been able to head to a baseball game—but now neither of them can. Obviously they can still do either one; they just have to have a conversation with their spouse.

Some of our old friends might get frustrated that we have to "ask permission." (We're not asking permission, of course—it just appears that way to those who have only known us as unmarried.) Most friends will be able to turn this corner with you; eventually, most friends who started out as his friends or her friends either become our friends or fade out of the picture.

If one of your friends does not like the person you have married, their role in your life will, and should, get smaller. If your friend doesn't respect your spouse, he or she will not be able to help you on your marriage journey, and you need to let that person go. This can be very difficult to do, especially when your old friend may have been so much a part of your life; but now that you are married, your spouse is your priority. Outside of your relationship with Jesus, your marriage relationship is the most important one in your life. Any relationship that poses a threat to your marriage must be let go.

"Do not be misled: 'Bad company corrupts good character'" (1 Cor. 15:33). I have heard it said, "Show me your friends, and I will show you your future." If we have a friend who is disrespectful to his or her spouse or jealous of our relationship with our spouse or unwilling to grow in his or her marriage, we can expect that over time the poor qualities that possess our friend will begin to possess us too. If we hang around bitter, disrespectful, unfaithful people, their habits eventually begin to corrupt our good character as well. We have to make conscious and sometimes difficult decisions to do life with people who are honoring God and honoring others.

Over the years, I have seen couples' friends have a huge effect on their marriages. There are two couples I have spoken to recently whose marriages were destroyed because of the negative influence of friends in their world. In both situations, one of the spouses spent hours every week with a group of people who were more interested in playing than in a life of responsibility and commitment—not the kind of friends we should spend hours with if we are trying to build our marriage.

Single people who hang out in clubs should not be your or your spouse's closest friends. Men and women who haven't the slightest idea what they are on the planet for should not be your or your spouse's closest friends. Without a sense of purpose, we all make pretty stupid decisions. I'm not saying that we shouldn't have people in our life who are at different places on life's journey. I'm just saying that it's not the wisest decision to share our most intimate relationship with them every single day.

Are you surrounding your marriage with people and other couples who are committed to marriage in general and to *your* marriage specifically? Will they help keep you on the path when you start to waver? Do you have a group of friends who, while they will listen to you, will not let you husband-bash or wife-bash indefinitely?

If you realize that you don't have very many married couples in your life who can be a support to you in your marriage, why don't you begin the process of cultivating some? Invite a couple to dinner or to coffee with you and your spouse. Join a small group at church for couples.

I have a great circle of friends. Some are single, and some are married. Some are newlyweds, and some have been happily married for years longer than I have. These are the ones I open my heart to for input and advice. These are the ones on whose shoulders I cry when my season of life seems overwhelming, the ones who can make me see the good in Philip when I can't.

I am in community with some pretty awesome people.

But I have to tell you that my friendships didn't happen randomly. I have built and continue to build them over the course of years. We have to *choose* to do life with people and continually press toward deeper levels of friendship and community. It's nice to have people in our life whom we don't have to perform for, don't have to pretend around; we all need people who give us the freedom to be ourselves but who love us enough to encourage our best self to come forward.

Real friendships take time. They require an investment of time over the long haul. Over time we discover the history of the people we do life with. We find out their stories, their struggles, their backgrounds and families, which leads us to understand the context from which they do life.

Real friendships take patience and forgiveness. The closer we get to people, the higher the potential for hurting each other—mostly unintentionally—which requires us to offer our friends the same grace and forgiveness we need from them when we mess up.

Real relationships with people who love us are worth every moment and every dollar.

I recently learned of a term called "collaborative divorce." It is a process that engages a team of experts to guide couples through the process of divorcing. A collaborative-divorce team might include attorneys, therapists and financial experts. Interesting. I understand and value the team concept, but I wonder how things might change if couples who opt for the cost and effort of a collaborative-divorce team put that same energy and care into restoring their marriage, perhaps with the help of a collaborative-marriage team (also called friends).

I do not believe that an unhappy marriage is doomed to divorce. All marriages, at some point, are unhappy. All marriages go through difficult times, but things can and often do change. There is plenty of research to show that, except in cases in which one of the spouses or the children are being physically abused, an unhappy marriage is better than a divorce for everyone involved.

In one study it was reported that 86 percent of unhappily married people who stuck it out found that five years later their marriages were happier. In fact, nearly three-fifths of those who rated their marriage "unhappy" in the late 1980s and who stayed married rated their marriage as either "very happy" or "quite happy" when they were re-interviewed in the early 1990s.

According to the study, the worst marriages showed the most dramatic turnarounds. If these couples achieved those results by simply not leaving, imagine what could happen if they made a deliberate effort to learn how to resolve their conflicts, to understand each other and to improve their communication![1]

Your friends should be part of your collaborative-marriage team. Allow them to do their part to see your marriage succeed.

Working to Live, Not Living to Work

> I have sacrificed everything in my life that I consider pre-
> cious in order to advance the political career of my hus-
> band. —Pat Nixon

I can't imagine that Pat Nixon's sacrifice was a good thing.

We live in the real world, so our marriages must thrive as we
navigate children, parents, our past, our friends and our careers.

Most of us have jobs. This is good! The challenge is to not let
our job cost our marriage. If we work so many hours a week that
we rarely get to spend time with our spouse, this will eventually
lead to a lack of intimacy, which will cause us to feel separated
from the one to whom we are supposed to be the most connected.

Of course, there are seasons in which more work is required.
If we are starting a new company, changing positions, planning a
conference or working on a special project, we might work more
hours than we normally do. Maybe while a wife finishes school,
her husband works days and she works nights for a few months.
Fine. But this can't become the new normal.

God did the work of creation for six days and took one to rest.
Making sure that we rest and connect with each other is crucial to
keeping our marriage strong. In our fast-paced world, this is not
always easy—but it is essential. There has got to be time set aside to
just *be*—time to stop going, going, going and doing, doing, doing.

On the flip side, there are some people who are so busy chasing
dreams that they won't get a regular job. In my city of Los Angeles,
many are waiting for their big break either in the entertainment
industry or in some other business venture. Dreams are important,
and they may be God-given, but if our lack of work is hurting our
family, change needs to happen.

Philip and I live together, work together and dream together.
It might seem as though we have lots of together time. However,
we have to be diligent about having couple time. Our life together
is so meshed with our call from God that if we are not conscious,
our hours together will be all about work.

When we are thinking about something new at church, or
when we are strategizing about how to cast vision for a particular

project, or when I am planning a GodChicks conference, more work time is required.

We understand that about each other.

But there are times when we must stop our work thoughts and pursue the other part of our purpose: to be a strong couple. There are times when I am at home that I need to take off my pastor-teacher hat and put on my wife-mother hat.

You probably have to do that too. I spoke with a young woman recently who was an executive in her company. She loved her work and was very passionate about it. All that is good. The problem is that she did not know how to chill out at home. She found it very hard to relax and to leave work at work. Not that we can't work from home sometimes, but she did it all the time. If she wasn't actually doing the work, she was talking about it. She couldn't—or, rather, she didn't—take off the super-executive hat and put on the wife hat. And this caused damage in her marriage.

Your husband doesn't want you to be his boss; he wants you to be his wife. Get good at switching hats. Your wife does not want you to be her boss either. You are her husband.

Hey, women, perhaps you are a stay-at-home mom, and that is your job, or you are working from home so that you can be with your young children. Great! The same rules apply. You still need to take off your work hat and your mom hat to make time for you and your husband to connect, even if it is only for a few minutes amid the chaos of a home with children. Maybe it's hard to go from watching *Blue's Clues* in your sweats and administering naptimes, mealtimes and playtimes to caring for your husband in non-mommy jeans and expressing yourself to him in a way that captures his heart. I know it's hard. But because you love him and he loves you, you have to do it. And while he loves the mom you've become, he still wants the playfulness and excitement of the woman he married.

And husbands, there will be times when you have to take off your work hat and be the man who pursued her. There will be times when she wants her "boyfriend." Sometimes you need to go back to doing what you did to get her.

A few years ago, I was trying to help a young couple navigate their marriage through a rough season. He was in school and working full time. She was also working, and they had a young child. Easy to see why they were having some challenges.

His solution to this busy season was to tell her and me that for the next year their marriage needed to be put on the back burner. I assured him that I understood what a busy season it was for them and that his wife certainly shouldn't expect date nights twice a week; however, if he was planning to put the marriage on the back burner for a year, he probably wouldn't have a marriage in a year. I suggested some other ways to handle their very busy life and ways to better their communication.

He wasn't really open to my suggestions. That's fine. Everyone is entitled to figure it out on his or her own or to find even better solutions. I don't know everything! But sadly, his solution—to ignore his wife for a year while he finished school—did not work. They were divorced by the end of the year.

Planted in the House of God

> The righteous will flourish like a palm tree, they will grow like a cedar of Lebanon; planted in the house of the LORD, they will flourish in the courts of our God. They will still bear fruit in old age, they will stay fresh and green (Ps. 92:12-14).

The Bible is clear: If we want our lives to flourish (and I imagine most of us do), we must be planted in the house of God. Planted. Not just attending, but planted, with roots going down, taking in nutrients, and with leaves sprouting, giving off oxygen.

Planted. Learning, growing and serving.

Planted. Not moving from church to church.

Planted. So that people know you.

Planted. So that people can hold you accountable to living the God life.

Planted. So that when life is hard, people know how to pray for you.

Planted. So that when life is good, people celebrate with you.

The Bible does not say that we will flourish if we have a great job, own a great house or live in a great neighborhood. No. It says that our life will flourish if we are planted in the house of God. All the good stuff, including a strong marriage, comes out of being planted in God's house.

My life revolves around being planted in the house of God. I don't just clock in and out as if attending church is an obligation or as if I am doing God a big favor. No. I am committed to the people in my world at Oasis. We are not just church friends. We call it doing life together. We are every-day, every-season kind of friends.

The theme song of the old sitcom *Cheers* says that we all want to go where we are known and where the people are glad we came. That's what happens when we are planted in God's house. We are known.

Maybe you are experiencing such pain in your relationship right now that loneliness is overwhelming you. You and I were created for relationship, so when there is a disconnect, we feel lonely and isolated. I have good news: "God sets the lonely in families" (Ps. 68:6). He brings the lonely, which is often you and me, into the house of God to connect with and to do life with His family! Connecting to a life-giving church is one of the best things we can do for our marriage.

Because I am planted in God's house, I am surrounded with people who are committed to making a difference on the planet. We are determined to build healthy marriages, because we realize that as our families get stronger, we become more equipped to make a difference in our world.

And that's why we are here! To bring light into dark places. Our churches and our marriages should be beacons of light that show those who are frustrated, hurt, lost and confused where to come for help and encouragement. Sometimes one of the best things we can do for our marriage is to get connected with a small group in our church that is reaching out into our community and into the world. Taking our eyes off our own pain for a moment to focus on helping people will bring new energy to our marriage.

It's important to remember that life will never be perfect. And in our distracting, imperfect world, it's easy to lose sight of the main thing in marriage: our spouse! We need to make a firm decision that throughout every season of our life, we will keep our relationship with our spouse as the most important one. Often we will have to shift the focus intentionally away from our children, our family, our past, our friends or our job back toward our marriage.

We can build strong, amazing marriages that impact our world—if we learn to do our one and only life well. And doing life well means learning to navigate the different pieces and parts of life. Doing marriage well means learning that, no matter what requires our attention in this moment, we will shift our attention back to what makes our marriage strong. Shifts must happen.

Think It Through

Women

1. Children are a wonderful addition to a family, but should they be the center of a marriage? Why or why not?
2. "Parenting is the procedure of teaching and training your children to leave your home and to begin lives of their own." Are you clinging to your kids, fearful of them ever leaving, or are you preparing them to build a life for themselves when they leave your home? What are some ways in which you can prepare them for mature adulthood?
3. Do your parents have more influence over you than your husband does? Does their input create division in your marriage? How can you take the best of what your parents taught you without letting their advice overtake you?
4. How do friends play a role in your marriage? Think about your closest friendships. Do those relationships build up your marriage or tear it down? (If it's the latter, creating new friendships might be in order!)

Men

1. Do you find yourself talking more about the business of family ("Who is cooking dinner?" "Who is picking up the kids?") than about the relationship of marriage? How can you reconnect with your wife this week to focus on building your relationship?

2. Remember Priscilla Shirer's story about how a train kept her and her husband awake all night? Did you live with anything (depression, bitterness, jealousy) before getting married that has come out in your marriage? Are you determined to not allow that "third person" from the past to invade your present? How will you deal with your past?

3. How can you and your wife invest in relationships with people who are seeking God's purpose? Do any specific people come to mind? Who and how can you reach out to them? It will take time and patience, but it will be worth it! (If you cannot think of anyone, try joining a small group at your local church to build new relationships.)

4. Besides Sunday mornings, what are you involved in at church? Start serving, start loving, start enlarging your perspective so that you and your spouse can grow together in God's purpose. He created both of you to make and to be a difference in a lost and broken world.

10

Give Me Five!

Philip

Men want the same thing from their underwear that they want
from women: a little bit of support, and a little bit of freedom.
Jerry Seinfeld

A man should fulfill his duty as a husband, and a woman should
fulfill her duty as a wife, and each should satisfy the other's needs.
1 Corinthians 7:3, *GNT*

Women often think, *What the heck do men want, anyway? What are
they thinking?*

Are they thinking?

Is it something mysterious? Is it too personal, or is it something
they've been waiting to tell you?

Women are often tempted in a silent moment to ask a man,
"What are you thinking?"

"Nothing."

Now her interest is piqued. "Come on, what were you thinking?"

"Nothing."

"Are you thinking about something that is personal and intimate, something you're hesitant to say to me?"

No. He probably isn't.

Men and women are different, as we have said a number of times already. The differences cause us to misunderstand what the other wants, expects or is interested in. In this chapter I'll first attempt to help women understand (a little bit, anyway) life through the eyes of the men they love. Then I'll address the men.

There are two major reasons many women struggle with relationships with men. One reason is the hurt and pain they have encountered in past relationships, which they can't seem to overcome. We spent time in the first chapter of this book addressing how to overcome wounds of the past, which I hope will help you navigate this struggle.

The second reason women struggle in relationships with men is that they don't know how to relate to or communicate with a man. I hope that this chapter will help you in this area.

There are reasons that men struggle in their relationship with women too. These involve communicating to a woman that she is the most important person in his life—expressing understanding and support of his wife's desires and dreams.

The High Five

I accidentally came up with a strategy for enhancing relationships during a counseling session with a married couple. This session got so complicated and so emotional that I got confused. I was lost. I had no idea what the real problem was or where to go next.

When they looked at me with expectation, waiting for my input about how to move forward, I could have said, "What do you say we order in some pizza, because this is probably going to take awhile?" I came very close. Counseling is not a gift of mine. Instead, I got an idea that has helped me with other couples—and has even helped Holly and me in our marriage. You might call this the help-me-help-you method (yet another *Jerry Maguire* reference), but I prefer to call it the high five of our marriage.

I asked the husband—we'll call him Dave, even though his real name is Rick—"Dave, I want you to tell me five things that you need from your wife, Janice [her real name is Janice], that will cause you to enjoy your relationship more. What do you need in order for your marriage to be closer to what you had hoped it would be?"

Then I asked Janice to do the same.

I also told them *not* to tell me five things that they wanted each other to start or stop doing—just five things that they needed. For instance, they couldn't say, "I need you to stop being an idiot," "I need you to close your mouth when you chew; it embarrasses me in front our friends" or "I need you to stop nagging me."

I wanted to hear admissions like,

"I need to know that you love me."

"I need to know that I am important to you."

"I need to know that you care about my feelings."

"I need to feel as if I can go out with my friends to have fun and not feel that you are jealous of my time."

Dave and Janice needed a bit of coaching to come up with their five needs.

Each time one of them expressed a need, I followed up with this question: "What can your spouse do to help you feel what you've described?" And then I asked the listening spouse, "Are you willing to do some or all of those things?"

The sequence went something like this:

"I need to feel that you care about the things I enjoy," Dave said.

"What do you think Janice can do to help meet that need?" I asked.

"When I talk about my work, you could seem as if you are interested," he continued.

I looked to Janice and asked, "Do you think you can try to do that during the next week?"

And because Janice is not a jerk, she responded, "Yes, I can try."

Finally, I asked Dave if he was willing to acknowledge Janice's effort when he saw her trying to meet his need.

These five things became their priorities for the next few weeks—their high five. And off they went with some very clear and helpful direction, which they had come up with on their own. When we met again, I focused on holding them accountable for their actions and priorities while helping to fine-tune their efforts.

What resulted was an immediate change in Dave and Janice's relationship. They also learned a method that they could turn to when things got messy (and in marriage, having messy moments is a given!).

The High Five for Men

A woman might feel like saying to her husband in frustration, "Just tell me what you want! Just tell me what to do." I can't answer for every man, of course, but from the various marriages I've observed over the years, I have a fairly good idea of what most men would say to this request.

Here are what I think are the five biggest needs of men. They are not in any order of priority. (The tricky part is that the man in your life may have a different list. That's where you come in. *Ask him*. Be a student of him. That said, I'm confident that these five will be somewhere in or near your husband's top 10.) These could be some of the most important things you could ever learn.

First High Five: Respect

A man likes to be with a woman who makes him feel respected. To be someone's hero, in some area of his life, is essential to a man's soul. Respect makes men feel as if we are moving toward hero status. But a woman can't have a hero she doesn't respect.

A man will thrive when he is respected. He will try, he will work, and he will overcome many obstacles if he is respected now and believes that there is more respect ahead. As coaching great John Wooden has said, "Respect a man, and he will do all the more."

Look at this issue from the opposite perspective: if a man feels disrespected, he will retreat. If he feels disrespected, this gap has to be repaired—even if he is totally in the wrong, is completely irrational or insensitive or is blind and oblivious to a woman's needs. Why? Because if a man feels disrespected long enough, he may retreat forever. He will become like the groundhog that comes up to see his shadow and then makes a hasty retreat to the safety of his hole in the ground. "I'm not going out there to be disrespected anymore." It is also hard for a man to ask for respect; to him, the need should be obvious.

Ladies, if your man retreats from you through his work or play or prefers to be with his friends rather than with you, take a serious look at this idea: *Maybe he does not feel respected by you*. Respect is the oil that makes a man's engine run smoothly. It helps us keep an open mind and heart. If you want to bring back the fire or keep the fire lit in your relationship, be brave enough to ask him some questions: "What do I do or say that causes you to feel respected?"

After you have asked, then listen. Really listen. Don't argue with his logic. Don't say, "That makes no sense." Instead, try this: "Thank you for sharing with me. I know that was probably not easy for you to tell me, and I appreciate your honesty." Then ask, "Is there anything I do that makes you feel disrespected?"

If he's honest and if you listen and if you then make changes in your actions, it will open your relationship up to a whole new level of trust and responsiveness.

On a related note: men like to win. They like to compete and to succeed. Most men retreat from a no-win situation.

A man who is not emotionally mature may express his desire to win by always wanting to be right, by being stubborn or by rarely admitting that he is wrong. An emotionally secure man also likes to win—and that's okay, because winning is good. But a mature man will apologize and admit that he has failed if he can see that doing so will get him a win. If he knows that you will forgive him, he will admit a failure or shortcoming—because making the relationship stronger is a win. But if he has learned through past experience that you will make him pay emotionally for apologizing, he won't admit so easily that he messed up. That feels a lot like a no-win situation.

Some men who are called prideful or arrogant really just don't want to be put in a situation in which they will be attacked, criticized or humiliated. A man wants to be with a woman who makes him feel good about himself and about life. How do you talk to your husband? What do you point out? If he thinks, *Others may criticize me, others may attack my efforts, but not my wife—she gets me; I can trust her*, then you have his heart.

Second High Five: Encouragement

Encouragement is important to a man. I addressed this earlier, but it is so important that it bears repeating.

Encourage him for who he is—a good leader, a good friend or a good support to you. Affirm his accomplishments. Support his efforts in the areas that are important to you, whether those are being a good father, being a faithful provider or being a better husband.

Someone somewhere came up with the notion that men should know how to barbecue, fix things around the house and assemble newly purchased furniture. When did that happen? When were they giving out those abilities? Apparently, I was absent that day. I relate to what comedian Paul Reiser says in his book *Couplehood*:

> When you actually move into a house, you learn quite quickly how little you know about anything. Day one, the guy comes to turn on the electricity. He asks me one question: "Excuse me, where is your main power supply?"
>
> Right there I'm stumped. First question as a homeowner, I had nothing.
>
> "I don't know. It's probably outside. Did you look outside, because I think I saw it there earlier.... Okay, I'm going to level with you, sir; I don't really know what a main power supply looks like. What is it? Is it a big thing? Maybe it's inside. It's definitely either inside or outside, I know that. Tell you what—why don't you find it, and that'll be your first little job. . . . You find it, I'll have it. That'll be what I do. You find it and do certain things with wires that I don't understand, and then I'll give you more money than you deserve. Is that fair?"[1]

Over the years I have learned who to call when something goes wrong. Holly tries to encourage me in this area, even though I don't give her much to work with: "Way to go, Philip. Way to call that repair guy. That was fast."

Her encouragement abilities really shine in other areas, however.

The first Sunday that we launched our church, Oasis, is a blank to me. It was a beautiful day—right up to the point I got to the podium. Then things kind of went downhill. I think. Like I said, I blanked it out.

That first Sunday we had about 60 people.

The second Sunday we had around 35.

The third Sunday we had just over 20. I calculated that I had about three weeks before I would be giving Holly a personal Bible study. (No one warned me not to focus too much on the first-day attendance; it's common for people to show up to wish you well with no intention of returning.)

Holly was serving as a member of our hospitality team—our greeters. I could imagine a Sunday very soon when she would say to me, "Hi, Philip! Welcome to The Oasis. I'm glad you came today. You are the pastor, so that's kind of important. I hope you give a great message today, because you're going to need it—and from the look of things, you're going to be the only one here to hear it, anyway."

Thankfully, that day never came, but she has never stopped encouraging me in my efforts as a pastor, a communicator and a leader. Starting Oasis Church was a long process; it took about 10 years to develop some strength and momentum behind our ministry. *Ten years!*

Holly encouraged me all the way. She encouraged my work and my investment in our ministry.

But she didn't stop there.

"You are a good dad, Philip."

"Really?"

Both my son and my daughter loved to play basketball, and they played on several teams over the years. Between my son and my daughter, I rarely missed a game. I missed a few meetings, rejected some invitations to speak and left the office early many days. There were things I did not do that could have advanced my ministry, but I rarely missed a game.

One afternoon after a long day at the office, even though I didn't really have the energy to do it, I went out to play basketball with my little son, Jordan. He was about six years old at the time. He would put his head down and drive to the basket—and crash right into my groin. A few inches higher and I'd be writing this book in a higher octave. Was this really necessary? Yes, it's part of the role.

"You are a good dad, Philip."

"Really?"

Children bring with them challenges to your leadership, questions you thought you'd never be asked, rebellious tantrums and much more. They have a way of making you feel as if they know a lot more about what's going on than you do. They stretch you to your limit.

"I don't think I know what to do next, Holly. It feels as if nothing I try gets through to them."

"You are a good dad, Philip. Most dads don't care that much or try this hard. Keep being there for them."

"Really? Okay. If you say so."

Holly's encouragement helped me believe that I could be a good dad and helped me become the dad I wanted to be.

Third High Five: Companionship

Does it surprise you to know that men want a woman who can be not only a lover but also a friend? Men want recreational companionship.

Guys love a woman who can carry on a conversation about business, hobbies or sports. In a way, she's like one of the guys—but she's also a lady. We love a woman who knows the meaning of "calling an audible," "hitting a grand slam" or "getting a triple double." Men love women who can do something that can make her like one of the gang—bowl, shoot pool, fish or play a game of ping-pong—while saying, "I'm a girl; give me a break." Women don't have to be able to do all of it—just enough of it.

I am not sure that Holly would ever have become a baseball fan if she weren't married to me. But because she loves me, she has learned quite a bit about the game. She recognizes players, knows what an RBI is and remembers who is about to break what record. And when she yells an intelligent comment at the umpire, it just warms my heart. Really. It lets me know that she is with me, fully engaged in an activity that is important to me.

What sport or hobby is your husband passionate about? Try learning something about it.

Men love to be with women who don't take themselves too seriously. Someone who sees the humor in life makes for great company. To be sure, we want a woman to have interests that have substance, to be honest and real. But a guy is overwhelmed and turned off by a woman who is too high maintenance, who makes every conversation too intense and weighty. While it's true that women should be treated as royalty, a woman who *needs* to be the center of attention all the time comes across as insecure, needy and demanding.

In contrast, a woman who is confident and playful is extremely attractive. There is no greater turn-off for a man than to feel as if the woman of his dreams is totally dependent on him for her every emotional need and has no life of her own. A guy knows that a girl with a full life, a life that doesn't revolve around him, won't get needy and possessive. She's more likely to be fun and to have something to say other than, "What are you really thinking?"

> Two tickets to a baseball game = $100
> A night out with the guys = $50
> Girls' night out = $75
> An enjoyable and confident companion = Priceless

A man also wants a companion who can provide domestic support. A woman may or may not be a great cook or someone who keeps the house spotless, but a woman who can add her touch to a home is a treasure. A good companion contributes her special something to the home.

Fourth High Five: Sex

Holly and I cover much more on the topic of sex in the next chapter, but I think it's important here to touch on the need of a man to be attracted to his wife. (I guess I could have used a better word here than "touch.") She does not have to have a perfect figure or dress like a supermodel to be sexually attractive to him. She does need to have a healthy appetite for sex, an ability to express passion and no inhibitions about making her desires known. Spontaneity, variety and enthusiasm get high marks in the heart of her husband.

A single woman should not sexualize her affection for the man she is dating. But there is an appropriate time in the relationship to begin expressing passionate feelings and a fearlessness about sex. This will reassure the man that he is pursuing a relationship with the right woman.

A woman who only has physical beauty going for her can't participate in a deep relationship—and an emotionally healthy man is looking for more than shallow, skin-deep attractiveness. He's looking for an articulate woman who has poise, purpose and intellect. And also someone he finds physically attractive.

"Attractive" is a fairly subjective concept; what's attractive to one man may be not so much to another. But being attractive to your husband will probably always be a factor in your relationship. That does not mean that you need to worry about aging and losing your beauty or that younger women everywhere are a threat to your marriage. It simply means that it's important to care about your husband's tastes. Find out what "does it" for him when it comes to your selection of clothes, your hairstyle and the amount of make-up you use.

Yes, you *are* more than your looks.

No, a man should not judge you alone on how you look.

It may be true that men fall in love through their eyes and women fall in love through their ears. As much as you desire to hear "I love you" and "You are special to me," he longs for you to present yourself in an attractive way.

Fifth High Five: Adventure

Most men love taking risks. They want to get involved in something that demands something of them that is a challenge.

The kind of challenge can vary a lot and depends on the guy. He may be interested in outdoor excursions, in starting a business or in learning about the latest technology gadget. Whatever the shape it takes, it's about conquering a mountain—a mountain that looks like writing a book, starting a new career, launching a ministry, taking a course at night school or traveling to another country.

The problem is that sometimes a man might attempt to scale that mountain regardless of who it may hurt, what the consequences are or even whether or not it's ethical. That is why it's important that he is guided by strong values—because he *will* want to take on a battle.

And he needs someone who will support his adventure.

Sometimes the woman he loves presents herself as the enemy of a man's adventure. Don't let that be you. Love him. Encourage him. Challenge his ethics and his wisdom. Point him to solid mentors. And support him.

After reading the high five of most men, you might be tempted to think, *Men are superficial.* They just want someone to have sex with and to play with, someone who is pretty and who will tell them how special they are.

Hmm . . . how can I say this? You are not far off.

But if instead of rolling your eyes you refuse to judge his needs and try to meet them, you may be shocked at his response. If you try to meet his needs, he will go all out for you. There is nothing he will not do for you, his treasure rediscovered.

I listed the top five needs of men as *respect, encouragement, companionship, sex* and *adventure*. Are these yours, men? Let your wife know.

Women have needs too. Her top five might be something like *non-sexual touch, conversation, honesty/openness, financial security* and *family commitment*. Talk to her and find out if these are her needs. And remember: she is not wrong for having needs that are different from yours.

If you commit yourself to meeting the needs of your wife, she will open up to you. She will trust you. She will put more effort into meeting your needs.

Our New York Story: A Moment of Glory

Holly loves romance. Holly loves to be shown that she is valuable.

I don't always get it right. Sometimes I feel "romantically challenged." But I get it right sometimes.

I think the basic theory of effective romance is that a lifestyle of ongoing, small romantic gestures is better than a one-time big event of romance. If you never show any romantic efforts until the anniversary comes around once a year, your big efforts won't have quite the same impact as a big effort surrounded by a lot of smaller efforts.

The grand gestures, of course, are a little less significant to a long-term relationship. These formerly romantic gestures now tend to fall into the category of the less than glamorous, such as a husband giving flowers after he blew it or giving a big gift to compensate for a stupid move or pleading, "I know I forgot our anniversary, but look at this dress I bought you."

But big romantic events can be powerful. And—may I point out—on one particular occasion I got it right.

Holly loves love stories. She loves the movie *Sleepless in Seattle*.

We have watched that movie many times. The whole story revolves around the story in another movie, *An Affair to Remember*, which is another love story. It's endless.

The basic plotline of *Sleepless in Seattle* has to do with misunderstandings or uncertainties in the relationship between the two main characters. They go through the challenges of any good story until finally it boils down to, "If you love me, meet me at the top of the Empire State Building."

I don't know how it happened, but I was just sitting there minding my own business when I started thinking about how much I love my wife, how special she is to me and how I should express the level of passion and value to her that the movie character did. So I got this idea and decided that I was going to recreate this same level of specialness that we had seen in her favorite story. I spent about two months planning and organizing the big event, and here's how it played out.

I told Holly one day that I needed to go into the office extra early the next morning. I would be leaving around six in the morning, so I would not be there when she woke up. Around eight the next morning, when she came into the kitchen, she found three envelopes on the table.

The first envelope simply read "Holly." She opened up the envelope to find a letter that said, "If you love me, meet me at the top of the Empire State Building." Also in the envelope was an airplane ticket to New York City. I had left early in the morning because I was already on an earlier flight to New York.

I told her in the note that I had our children's care organized, including who was taking care of them, who was staying where overnight and so forth. I had planned a ride for her to get to the airport. I had a hotel booked. I wrote that we were going to have a couple days to get away and to enjoy each other.

A note inside the second envelope said, "Don't just stand there—you've got two hours to pack and get out of here."

The third envelope said, "Do not open until you are on the plane." In this envelope (although I did not have much confidence that she would wait until she got on the plane to read it), I just wrote a note that told her how much I loved her and that I was looking forward to spending a few special days away with her. And I signed my name. I thought this was important, because I didn't want anyone else to get credit for my moment of glory.

Holly says that when she got on the plane, she was so excited that she was telling everyone around her what was happening. This does not surprise me.

I had arranged a limo to meet her at the airport in New York. The limo driver was standing there in the airport with her name on the card when she got off the plane, and he played the soundtrack to *Sleepless in Seattle* in the limo on the way to the hotel. He took her to the hotel to drop off her luggage and then drove her to the Empire State Building.

I planned all this out assuming that she did love me and that she did want to meet me at the top of the Empire State Building—unlike the hero in the movie, who, in my opinion, left too much up to speculation.

Holly and I had a great few days. I was a hero. I knocked the ball out of the park. It was a huge victory. It was like winning the World Series.

I even planned things for us to do while we were in New York. I had planned things that I knew she would enjoy, like having dinner at a nice restaurant, going to a Broadway play, getting tickets to the David Letterman show and attending a Yankees game. I planned *only* the things I knew she would enjoy.

Now the way Holly is, the more she tells a story, the bigger, more creative and more emotional it gets. Sometimes she'll tell a story, and I'll think, *Was that actually me in that story? I don't remember it that way at all. Did you go a second time when I was not included? Because I don't think I was the same guy who went with you on that one. Your version seems different to me—I don't really remember King Kong hanging off the building.*

But in this situation, it worked out for me. Our trip to New York has been a gift that keeps on giving, because she likes to tell the story again and again, and when she tells it, she relives it. Even though it's been almost 15 years since we took that trip, it's as if I did the whole thing over again last month. And when she retells the story and re-experiences it, she gives me the "look" that tells me she is *so* glad that I'm the man in her life!

Separating the Men from the Boys

A phenomenon of our day is the confusion many men feel about who they are supposed to be. Am I supposed to be strong and tough or sympathetic and creative? Which one of those am I being right now? Am I really a man? Do I need to change something about how I handle things to be a genuinely grown-up man?

The apostle Paul wrote, "When I was a child, I talked like a child, I thought like a child, I reasoned like a child. When I became a man, I put the ways of childhood behind me" (1 Cor. 13:11).

Putting away childish things. What is that exactly?

Paul mentions the way he spoke and the way he thought. But I believe that if others are going to see changes in our thoughts and words, there has to be change deep in our soul.

One of the most recognizable parables Jesus told is the story of the prodigal son. This story reveals some distinct qualities that I believe can help men sort out the confusion they feel about what it means to be a man.

At its heart the story is about our Father in heaven. Jesus uses a story to reveal something about the heart of God—and about the kind of man every man should aim to be.

Men often drift toward one of two extremes. They lean toward being weak, self-occupied and passive or toward being tough, mean and difficult.

The Passive Guy

Let's look first at the youngest son, the prodigal, who typifies the first extreme. He's the one who wastes his life away and finally returns home.

He's self-absorbed. He's selfish. He thinks, *I want mine now. I want to do my own thing. I want to be free.* Before he comes to his senses, before he realizes that he needs to make some changes if he wants to be a real man, he is passive. It shows in the way he thinks and talks. He has no goals. He has no direction. He likes to party. He wants to hang out with the boys. His life is going nowhere, and he's looking for someone to enable him to keep it up.

In our world, this kind of male is common—we see him all the time. He's the kind of guy we can't rely on. He doesn't step up to the plate when we need him. He doesn't speak up for what's right.

We see this situation with Adam and Eve in the Garden of Eden. When the serpent came to tempt Eve, to steal humanity's birthright and to take our blessing, we have no evidence that Adam ever did anything to prevent disaster. He didn't step between Eve and the serpent and say, "Wait a minute, Eve, this is wrong. Let me intervene; let me defend you. Let me defend the garden, our future and our relationship with God." His wife ate the forbidden fruit, and then Adam ate.

Adam was passive; he abdicated his responsibility.

We see a lot of men like the prodigal son in our churches. They are little boys in men's bodies. They are young boys who are in their 20s and 30s—and even in their 40s. They may look like 30-year-old men, but they're still not sure what they want to do with their life. They are still adolescents. They can't keep a job, and if they have one, they work part-time.

I realize that there are seasons in life in which there is a need for training and preparation. A man may go to school or might intern for a year or two. But for some guys this becomes a lifestyle. They can live a decade or two that way.

It's not uncommon to see a group of guys—13 roommates—who each pay twenty-seven dollars to cover the rent. That way no one has to work much. This approach gives them plenty of time to play Wii and X-Box, express their art and go surfing on the weekend. Some of these guys would rather stay up until 2 AM writing "love songs to God" than do something that will make a difference in their life and in the world. How about being a provider? How about being a strong advocate for someone who needs you? How about setting an example of dependability and trustworthiness to the next generation?

I'm convinced that *boredom* is the reason some guys get addicted to porn! They have nothing else going on in their lives. Pornography and fantasy relationships are easier to build than real, lasting relationships.

It's difficult to get up at eight in the morning for a men's prayer gathering when you've been up until three playing video games and updating your Facebook page. He signs up for a class, but he can't even attend three sessions in a row because he can't keep his life organized. It's weak. It's what boys do with their lives. "I just wanna hang out and be cool. Don't put pressure on me, man. You're stressing me out."

Sometimes I wonder if this guy's secret desire is to marry a woman who has a really good career and a nice house, because then he can keep pursuing his dream while she brings home the money.

If someone challenges him to do more with his life, his feelings are hurt. He would probably get mad reading my comments—but then again, he is probably too passive to read a book about personal improvement. But here you are reading this book. Just doing that puts you in a completely different realm.

Now don't get me wrong. This guy is a nice guy. We love this guy. We all like having him around. But the reality is that he rarely steps up to the plate. He does not make tough decisions. He tends to excel at making *no* decisions, because he doesn't want anybody not to like him. At the end of the day, he abdicates responsibilities.

It's like following someone on the freeway whose right-hand turn signal is blinking. It has been blinking for 17 miles. You think, *Okay, this guy has the potential to turn right at some point. But I have no idea if he's actually going to make a turn or not. Should I slow down, should I speed up, should I go around him?*

The danger in this situation is that some of the women we care so much about have fallen for these kinds of guys. I think some women confuse the love between a mother and a son and the love between a wife and a husband.

Ask yourself, *Do I want my sons to be like the man I love? Do I want my daughters to marry someone like him?* Because that man will impact your children and set an example that they will follow.

When men who are still little boys get married, a problem is brewing. It's difficult for a boy to become a man overnight. He often hurts his wife because he doesn't know how to be there for her. It's disappointing for a woman when a man does not know how to be strong.

Sometimes aggressive or gifted women are drawn to men like this because they can tell these guys what to do—and the men will do what they are told. I must caution you that I've seen many women like this in the counseling office who now despise their husbands for the same weaknesses that first attracted them.

Passive men need to come to their senses, as the prodigal son did. They need to recognize what has influenced them and what example they have been following. They need to meet other guys who are doing something with their lives.

At the end of the day, they need to take action. Take some initiative. Create some momentum! Attend a class about business or ministry. Develop a special skill. Meet other men who are moving in similar directions in business, faith or ministry. It's extremely important to engage in productive activities and events with other men who are an example of strength.

If you are the wife of one of these men, encourage and provide opportunities for him to spend time with men of strength who are doing something with their lives. It is their influences that will help him become the man he was created to be instead of the little boy who needs to grow up.

The Aggressive Guy

Now let's look at the other extreme: the older brother. He typifies a desperate and insecure masculinity.

He is the critical guy. He's angry. He's hostile. He criticizes people. He's the tough guy. He thinks that anything sensitive or compassionate is girl stuff. He's not comfortable with hugging, kissing or crying.

If he were religious, he'd be the guy who knows all the rules. He'd be the guy who excels at keeping track of what everyone else did wrong. He's the rule-focused person who doesn't have the heart of the Father at all.

Real men can laugh, cry, fight for something, win and overcome disappointment. We can do *all* that. We don't have to be one or the other of these guys. We can be both. We can be both strong and compassionate.

This older brother likes to boss everybody else around. He wants to give people orders. He doesn't want be *under authority*; he wants to be *in power*. His leadership is reliant on a title or a position.

These men are boys who don't want to take direction from anyone. They don't like people with a badge. They criticize their leaders—the boss, the employer, the pastor and anybody else who has authority.

He thinks, *If I were in charge, things would be different around here.*

Well, you're not in charge. That's because you're a jerk. Nobody trusts you. You earn trust by coming under authority and demonstrating that you are trustworthy.

Sometimes this is a military man or policeman or security guard. While I have great respect for people serving in these careers, some men are attracted to these positions because it offers a veneer of strength. Yet they often can't take the strength they learn on the job and put it into real-life relationships.

Many years ago, a man we will call Darryl came to me. He asked if I would give him counsel as his pastor. He told me his story and his concerns. After I thought about what he'd told me, I gave him my input—and it hurt his feelings.

He was a difficult person to talk to for about a year after that. He was pouting. A grown man.

I thought, *Come on, you asked for my opinion, and I gave it to you. You're supposed to be tough and strong. Put your strength into humbling yourself and growing up.* But his version of strength produced separation of friendships and broken relationships. That isn't strength at all.

He was a pretender.

Ladies, are you involved with a pretender? Men, are you being a pretender? I hope not.

These men want to be strong but don't know how, so they get angry and intimidate people they can control, and they criticize people they don't understand. They scare their wives and intimidate their children.

What kind of man threatens his family? What kind of man scares his wife and kids? Can you imagine the prodigal son seeing his father running down the road toward him and thinking, *Oh no, here comes my dad—everybody duck. Put on a helmet!*

In the story we can see the older brother's lack of true spirituality. He says to his father, "Dad, how could you throw this party? This son of yours . . ." Isn't that interesting? He's talking about his own brother, but he calls him "this son of yours." "This son of yours is messed up, Dad. He spent all your money on prostitutes."

Mean-spirited people judge and jump to conclusions. I don't read anywhere in the story that the prodigal spent money on prostitutes. This idea comes out only in the older brother's accusations. That's what aggressive men do when they don't feel strong: they attack others.

Jesus taught us about laying our lives down to serve others. *That* is real strength.

The father in the story is strong—if only the older brother would apply himself to becoming like his dad! It's sad that the older brother says, "I've been here all this time," as though he is entitled to something because of tenure. In reality, he looks nothing like his father and has therefore disqualified himself. The older brother thinks he deserves something special, but he hasn't lived like the father has at all.

The father is strong; he rises to the need of every situation.

He is supportive and releasing of his younger son: "You want to leave? I'll let you go." He has concern and love for his son, but in his wisdom, he releases his boy.

He is compassionate; when his son returns, the father embraces him. He welcomes him home.

Men need to be able to express to those they love, "I love you whether you succeed or fail." Men also need to hear these words. Many men never heard this kind of love and endorsement expressed by their fathers.

Even Jesus needed to hear the endorsement of His father. God spoke out of the heavens and declared, "This is my dearly loved Son, who brings me great joy" (Matt. 3:17, *NLT*). Jesus then carried out His ministry with that declaration planted firmly in His heart.

If you are a single woman and considering a particular man with whom to build a life-long relationship, I encourage you to consider these examples of men that I've presented to you. Does the man you are considering lean toward the passive or the aggressive? Is he more of a man or more of a boy?

If you are married, what you have just read will help you to recognize the man with whom you are trying to communicate. As you think about the five needs of men, remember that they will look a little different for each man depending on whether he leans toward being passive or aggressive. Since we are assuming that you are in a relationship in which both you and your husband want to continue to grow emotionally, then at least a conversation about these issues, without making your husband feel attacked or criticized, would be helpful for you to have.

Think It Through

Women

1. How easy or difficult is it for you to communicate with your husband? Do you know what makes him tick? Ask your husband for his high-five list. Then be willing to try doing the five things he would like you to do. Give him your high-five list too.

2. "To be someone's hero, in some area of his life, is essential to a man's soul." How do you make your husband feel that he's your hero? What makes him feel respected? Disrespected?

3. How surprised would your husband be if you found out some stats about his favorite sports team or showed interest in his favorite hobby? Try it, and see what happens!

4. Do you support your husband's adventures, or does he feel as if you're the enemy when it comes to the mountains he wants to conquer in his life? What shape do your husband's adventures take? How can you both challenge and support him in his endeavors?

5. Does your husband lean at all toward being either passive or aggressive? What are some affirming ways in which you can help him as he seeks to be both a strong and compassionate man?

Men

1. Communication between men and women isn't always easy! Do you find it difficult to express to your wife how you feel about her? How can you better communicate to her your support of her dreams and her purpose in life?

2. Your wife may not always understand how best to communicate with you either. You can help her be aware of your needs and desires by telling her your high-five list. Ask her for hers too, and be willing to try doing the things she would like you to do.

3. What are some characteristics of a real man? How do you, as the apostle Paul said, put childish ways behind you? How are you endeavoring to grow as a man deep within?

4. Do you have any tendencies toward being passive, like the prodigal son, or toward being aggressive, like the older brother? What steps could you take to surround yourself with other men who are moving in healthy directions and who can encourage you to grow both in strength and compassion?

11

S-E-X Is Not a
Four-Letter Word

Philip+Holly

You and I, for the last twenty years,
have been fed all day long on good solid lies about sex.
C. S. Lewis, *Mere Christianity*

I learned in church that sex is the most awful, filthy thing on earth
and you should save it for someone you love.
Unknown

Always be enraptured with her love.
Proverbs 5:19, *NKJV*

We have good news for you: God wants you to have an incredible
sex life. Sex is a gift from God to us.

We're not sure where you got your information on sexual
intimacy. Maybe you got some of it from all those wonderfully
romantic movies, and now you are realizing, *Wait, that's not how it
went for me!* Rather than the perfectly choreographed movement
between two people who know exactly what they are doing, with
musical accompaniment and soft-focus photography, your experience with sex has been more along the lines of "Ouch! Honey,

your elbow is on my hair" and "Move over, I'm falling off the bed!" and "Remember what you did last time? Don't do that" or "You're crushing me. It's not that you weigh so much, it's just an awkward position." (And have you noticed that in the movies sex is never messy? Why does no one ever need a towel? What's with that?)

Maybe we can conclude that the movies are not the best place to get sex education.

There is a lot of false and discouraging information about sex. When Holly and I were going through pre-marriage counseling, I was 30 years old, and Holly was about 22, and we read an article about sexual fulfillment in marriage. This article said that women reach their sexual peak between the ages of 30 and 35 years of age. In the same article, we read that men reach their sexual peak between the ages of 18 and 23. I thought, *Oh great! I've peaked, and she hasn't even started yet.*

There are a lot of ideas out there about sex that confuse people.

So many couples we talk to have had horrible experiences with sex. Maybe she was abused sexually and comes into the marriage carrying scars, or perhaps he was promiscuous and now questions how he can rid his mind of the memories of others. We regularly pray with couples in which one person has a sexually transmitted disease that they are now bringing into the marriage.

It's common for a high percentage of couples to experience frustration and disappointment sexually on their honeymoon. If this includes you, it's probably a little embarrassing to admit.

Was that it?

Was that the best he had to offer?

Is that as passionate as she is going to be?

Are we going to have a lifetime of this kind of sex? Help!

It seems as if great sex should be so natural and easy to express. The good news is, it should get better. A lot better. And the even better news is, it will take practice. A lot of practice.

The bad news is it takes work, patience, understanding, trial and error, humility and honesty, as well as some other things that we will talk about in this short chapter.

Perhaps you were one of the very few people on the planet raised by incredibly functional parents who not only loved you but also loved each other emotionally and physically. They readily explained everything you needed to know about sex and answered all your questions openly, lovingly and without shame. On top of that, you and your spouse were virgins when you got married and thus entered marriage with no past baggage or relational hang-ups. On your honeymoon sex was perfect because you were so well prepared and knew exactly how to please each other.

If all the above is true, you can skip this chapter.

However, if you laughed with astonishment that we could even imagine that there are parents like that, because you are pretty sure those parents are mythical, or if you got your sex education from your friends, who were *so* well informed, or if you, like many people, indeed had a sexual past that you brought with you into marriage, then this chapter is for you.

When I (Philip) was a boy, my dad began his first father-son talk with me by calling me into his office. Already I knew I was in trouble.

Let me explain just a little. My dad was a conservative Baptist evangelist who specialized in preaching on the exact temperature of hell and emphasizing the anger of God. We had never discussed sex on any level in our house.

On this day, which *should* have been the beginning of many great conversations to prepare me for one of the best parts of marriage, my dad called me into his office.

He had written the f-word on a piece of paper. He showed it to me and asked, "Do you know what this means?" Now I *knew* I was in trouble. I assured him that I did not know what the word meant. Furthermore, I had never done it nor ever said it to anyone. I thought that response should just about cover my defense.

He went on to explain the activity, but his description actually sounded gross to me. I told him that I would never do that. (I later changed my mind.)

As you might guess, Dad left out a few details. I guess I was supposed to fill in the blanks by talking to my friends, whose parents had also given them a minimum amount of information.

After a few months of marriage, with this comprehensive sex education under my belt, it should have come as no surprise that one night (after what I thought was a passionate expression of sexual intimacy) I said to Holly, "That was pretty good, wasn't it?" and she gave me a half smile.

Not the response I was looking for.

She gave me the half smile that means, "I'm not trying very hard to hide my true feelings." And there was a little too much silence. I could tell I was in trouble. I had no idea what for, but I somehow knew that we were about to have a very uncomfortable conversation. (I'm sharing this with you, but please keep it to yourself. It's embarrassing.)

When Holly broke the news that it hadn't been the most exciting eight and a half minutes she'd ever had, I was shocked. "What? That wasn't enjoyable?" I figured that if I was having a good time, everyone in the room would be happy. Nope. Basically, the newness had worn off. It was time to deliver. *Deliver what?*

How was I to know? I had never asked. I had never had the father-son conversations that should have been ongoing and would have given me an idea of how to relate sexually to my wife.

It was a painful discussion, but that conversation with my new wife launched what has become a wonderful journey, an ongoing conversation that has lasted over 25 years and has produced a better sex life than I'd ever imagined. But at first it was, well, difficult.

I overreacted, got defensive, became insecure and didn't much enjoy having sex on many occasions—and even wondered what the fuss was all about. I thought, *Sex is not that great.*

Before we dig into the topic of sex, we want to let you know that we are very aware of people (like you, perhaps?) who have suffered sexual abuse. It makes us angry on your behalf that something designed to be wonderful between a husband and a wife may cause you pain or stand in the way of a fulfilling and healthy sex life. We are so sorry, and our word of encouragement to you is that there is a way to wholeness. It is important for you to get help. There are many places you can find that help—wise counselors, good books and churches with programs that can lead to your freedom. Don't stay bound another day. Life is too precious for that! Sex is a God-given gift and is meant to be enjoyed!

The Sexual Prerequisite

Let us say now, so that there is no misunderstanding, that we believe the Bible's instruction on sex. Sexual intimacy and expression are for a man and a woman who are married.

We also realize that in our world today, many people assume that single people who are dating are sexually intimate. Most think abstinence is an odd and unnatural standard. A majority of people think virginity is a condition to be remedied as soon as possible. Instead of virginity being a badge of honor, it is a reason for ridicule.

But we believe that sex is God's creation and that we should follow His directions on it. Being married obviously doesn't guarantee great, passionate, enjoyable and heart-pounding sex. There are other essential elements to great sex. But if you want to have God's blessing, you have to start with being married. Sex is designed for marriage. This view has not hindered us or hurt us in any way. We enjoy the passion of sex.

Singles should look forward to enjoying this level of intimacy and save this important part of their body and soul for their future spouse. The gift of virginity to our spouse is a rare but treasured gift.

There is power in purity. "Purity" means "uncontaminated and undiluted. Something that is uncontaminated and undiluted usually signifies power. There is power and great value in *pure* dedication, *pure* strength and *pure* gold.

None of us can go back and change our past, but we can go the rest of the distance with purity as our standard. When we choose purity, we declare that we value others, we demonstrate a self-control that can be trusted and we protect our relationships from physical and emotional disease.

In Greek mythology the Sirens' song is an interesting parallel to sexual desire. The Sirens were creatures who had the head of a female and the body of a bird. They lived on a rocky, dangerous island and, with the irresistible sound of their song, lured those who sailed near them to destruction on the rocks.

The Argonauts escaped the Sirens, because when he heard their song, Orpheus realized the peril they were in. He took out his lyre and sang a song so clear and ringing that it drowned out the sound of those lovely, fatal voices.

When Odysseus's ship passed the Sirens, he ordered the sailors to stuff their ears with wax so that they would not be able to hear the alluring power of the song. Odysseus, however, wanted to hear their beautiful voices, so he had the crew tie him to the mast. The Sirens sang as Odysseus's ship passed by their island. Their words were even more enticing than their melodies. They promised knowledge, wisdom and a quickening of the spirit to every man who came to them. The song was more beautiful than Odysseus had imagined! His heart raged with longing for the Sirens, but the ropes held him to the mast, and the ship sailed to safer waters.

The allure of sexual experiences is enticing and difficult to resist. When we are sexually aroused, reason often goes out the window; and unless we are bound by our convictions, we can be destroyed. Just as Orpheus sang a song so clear that it overrode the Sirens' song, we too must have a stronger song in our hearts to guide us along our sexual journey. We need to hear a song that will drown out the song sung by our society today.

The truth is that sex, which should be a gift to our life, will be a curse if it is not treated in the right way. While many people may not respect the biblical view of sex, our society's approach is not working.

Chlamydia and gonorrhea are two of the most commonly reported infectious diseases in the United States. The long-term consequences of these diseases can be life threatening and certainly life destroying.[1] More than one million people in the United States are living with HIV.[2] One-third of the pregnancies in the United States are unplanned and unwanted, and half of those will end in abortion.[3] Obviously, the way we are teaching and talking about STDs, AIDS and pregnancy is not effective, and the continual distribution of free condoms is not helping. There must be a better way.

There are dozens of magazines on grocery-store shelves that offer articles such as "How to Have Hot Sex with Your Boyfriend." Sadly, the vast majority of these are written by young women who haven't built lasting marriages.

We live in a society that practically obligates us to sexualize any feeling that comes along in our mind. Songs are filled with sexual passion. Movies present people who treat their sexuality as something that should be shared with whomever they are with at the moment. The idea is promoted that any limitations we put on our sexual expression are indications of a sexual hang-up. But the freer our world gets, the more sexually messed up we become. There are more sex addicts, sex offenders and sexually frustrated people than ever.

Great sex is not about how many people we have intercourse with but rather about the intimacy that occurs in a marriage when two committed people join hearts and bodies—the intimacy that occurs over the years. Although sex isn't the only part of a marriage, it is certainly an important one, for several reasons.

Reasons for Great Sex

For Enjoyment!

We will spend a lot of time in this chapter talking about the enjoyment of sex. "As a loving deer and a graceful doe, let her breasts satisfy you at all times; and always be enraptured with her love" (Prov. 5:19, *NKJV*).

Sex should be fun. Both the man and the woman should experience physical pleasure and should touch each other emotionally at a deep level. The average person thinks that Christians are uptight and sexually repressed simply because we have convictions about guidelines for sex. But emotionally and sexually healthy Christians experience passionate, uninhibited, hot, laugh-out-loud, heart-stopping and jaw-dropping sex!

We can't take ourselves so seriously. We have to laugh a little and play a little. This is an enjoyable part of life. We get to learn. We get to practice again and again. Sometimes we get it right and sometimes not so much—but we get to try it again tomorrow!

To Create Unity

"Therefore shall a man *leave* his father and his mother, and shall *cleave* unto his wife: and they shall be one flesh" (Gen. 2:24, *KJV*, emphasis added). A man is to *leave* his parents and join with, adhere to, cling to, *cleave* to his wife. To truly create unity in a marriage, we must leave all other options behind, whether they are emotional, mental or physical. The only person whose emotional needs we should be meeting, other than our children, is our spouse. Don't get exhausted trying to meet anyone else's. To create a unified marriage, we must leave the past and all others behind.

Sex is a unifying bond between husband and wife. It solidifies our union. When the rest of the world might seem crazy, when others hurt or betray us, it is wonderful to feel connected with our spouse. Often after a disaster many couples make love, because the experience reaffirms their life and their union. They are saying, in essence, *We are okay; we are together; we are alive.* Sometimes we have a really rough day—a coworker takes credit for our work, someone cuts us off in traffic and points a finger at us (and I am not talking about the index finger!), we run out of gas on the freeway. If we can come home and have sex with our spouse, the significance of those mishaps will fade—because we'll remember that someone is on our side.

We are not saying that sex solves all problems or that communication isn't crucial—but it does create a sense of unity. Sex was created to be a unifying bond, and withholding it should never be used as a weapon or as punishment.

To Produce Children

God commanded Adam and Eve to be fruitful, to multiply and to replenish the earth (see Gen. 1:28). (That's probably the only command that humans have had no trouble keeping!) So, yes, sex can and often does result in children. And we want that—but for too many couples, reproduction is the main purpose of sex. The fact that they have kids proves that they have been sexually active, but there is no unity, harmony or pleasure involved. Instead there is anger, hurt, frustration and misunderstanding. Those are not the qualities of great sex.

Qualities of Great Sex

Good Communication

First, we have to be willing to talk with each other about our thoughts, fears and feelings. We have to be willing to talk about what we like and what we don't like. And we must be willing to listen without being insecure and without rejecting the desires and concerns of our mate.

We know a couple that conducts marriage seminars. They talk about the number of women who complain to them about being frustrated sexually. Many women say that they've never or rarely experienced an orgasm but are afraid to discuss it with their husbands. They are afraid because whenever they have attempted to discuss it in the past, they've been humiliated by accusations from their insecure husbands, who blame them for the problems.

Their husbands aren't safe to talk to. These wives walk away from the conversation feeling, "There's something wrong with me." Some women even fake their enjoyment so they won't have to endure a difficult encounter with their husbands—but deep down they are frustrated.

Sex is more than knowing where the parts go. Great sex takes open and honest dialogue about what you want and need. And it takes leaving egos and pride at the door—easier said than done. If you really want your sexual relationship to get better and better, there needs to be an atmosphere in which both of you are free to share your feelings and needs without being embarrassed. Getting defensive will not help. When your spouse is sharing a need or a concern about your sexual relationship, listen. You are designed to meet each other's sexual needs—no one else can.

We heard a story about a man who had a difficult time talking about sex. Actually, he had a difficult time talking about a lot of things. He decided to go to Toastmasters to build his confidence and his communication skills.

In one exercise at the Toastmasters meetings, each person had the opportunity to speak for five minutes on a topic that was chosen randomly for them by drawing a three-by-five-inch card. One night when it was this man's turn, he drew a card that that had one word written on it: "sex." His job was to talk to the small audience of Toastmasters about sex—for five whole minutes. He gave his best attempt.

When he got home that night, his wife asked him, "What was your topic tonight at Toastmasters?"

Fearing that if he told her, it would lead to more questions and more awkward discussion, he stuttered, "I spoke about . . . s-s-s-s-sailing. Yeah, my topic was sailing." He sighed with relief, knowing that he had avoided a difficult conversation.

The next day the man and his wife went to the local mall. She went into a clothing store, while he waited outside. In the store his wife ran into one of the ladies that she and her husband both knew and who also attended Toastmasters.

The lady said, "I heard your husband speak at Toastmasters last night." She grinned slyly and continued, "Sounds as if he *really* knew his subject."

His wife thought for a minute and replied, "He doesn't know that much about it. He's only had the experience twice. The first time he got so sick that he threw up. The second time things got so wild that his hat blew off, and he never did find it."

Direct and honest communication about sex or any other topic will help us avoid misunderstandings. It is important that we communicate with each other about what turns us on, what turns us off and what our expectations are. Keeping the lines of communication open is crucial for making the sex part of life great. Just communicate.

Honesty

Honesty is another quality of great sex. Ask questions like "What have I done that you like?" and "What have I done that you don't like?" and "What makes you uncomfortable?" Questions like these, and honest answers to them, go a long way toward building understanding and unity.

Many couples are frustrated about their sex life because they are dishonest with each other about their feelings, desires and expectations.

Our culture struggles with our opinions and responses to homosexuals who "come out of the closet," but married people need to be honest (come out of the closet!) with their spouse. Let your spouse know what you desire. Be honest about temptations, orgasms and what you like or don't like. Many are fearful that if they tell their spouse what they like, he or she will get mad or think they are weird.

For a man sexual pleasure is fairly straightforward. Not so for women. And that is God's design. Because while sex is certainly fun and pleasurable, it is designed to create intimacy—and intimacy is not always straightforward. God did not make women like men; He certainly could have, but He didn't. He made the sexual needs and desires of women a little more complicated. Any male can go out and have one-night stands with multiple partners; it takes a man to do the work of creating intimacy.

It may be tempting for a woman to fake her reactions or responses. She may tell herself that she does it to avoid damaging her husband's ego, but more often it is because she is not being honest about what she needs. Don't fake it. You are not helping him figure out how to make it great for you if you fake it. You have years to figure it out together, so make sure that you are honest. He wants to get a win in this area, so lovingly and patiently be open and honest about what feels good and what doesn't. It is unfair to your husband and to you for you to build up resentment toward him because of sexual frustrations you have never shared.

While a wife may be dishonest about her sexual fulfillment and her enjoyment of having an orgasm, husbands can be dishonest about the importance of physical attraction. "No, I don't mind that you've gained 50 pounds. It's just more of you to love." A man who says that really loves his wife a lot; he is trying to make her feel good about herself—but it is usually at the expense of his own sexual enjoyment.

A woman climbs into bed with her hair in rollers, flannel pajamas on and an I'm-going-to-sleep-in-a-couple-minutes look on her face and then wonders why he doesn't show more passion about their sex life. She's thinking, *You love me for who I am on the inside, right?* Well, of course he does—but it is much easier to express that love when she presents herself in a way that is attractive to him.

Generally, men are visual creatures. God made them that way. Not that women don't appreciate a good-looking guy—they just don't tend to be motivated sexually all the time by what they see, whereas men usually are.

I (Holly) have a few thoughts to share. When Philip and I are out walking, we often notice couples. Sometimes we spot a beautiful woman with an average-looking guy, and Philip will ask, "How did *he* get *her*?" Every time, my answer is the same: "Philip, while looks matter to us, what is more important is how we are treated. That average-looking guy must be great at loving her, and that is how he got her!"

This is great news for millions of men!

Women are different in this way. Men are stimulated by what they see, which is why I do the best I can with what I have to make myself attractive. I want Philip to be attracted to me even when I am

82! I am the only woman my husband is going to have sex with, so I want to make it easy for him. It would be selfish of me to let myself go. I'm not going to get neurotic about it, but I will do the best I can with what I have.

If you have gained a significant amount of weight since your wedding day, I gently suggest that you work on a plan to get rid of it. *Of course* he loves you—and because you love him, you will work on becoming the healthiest you can. It is not about you looking like a supermodel; it is about you being the best you that you can be.

And if you are still wearing those flannel footie pajamas you had in high school, you should probably get rid of them. Unless he thinks they are attractive. He probably doesn't, but ask him. Ask, because he is motivated by what he sees. Take him with you to the lingerie store, and see what he thinks is sexy. You might be surprised. Why wouldn't you wear what he likes? Obviously you don't have to wear the scratchy lace bustier all the time, but put on something he thinks is sexy, and see what happens!

With those thoughts in mind, both of us realize that because we are committed to building our marriage, we have years to work it all out. Patience, in addition to honesty, is a good quality for great sex. If one particular sexual encounter with your spouse leaves lots to be desired, then talk about it and look forward to the next practice session! Sex probably isn't going to be a perfect 10 every time. Take the pressure off by relaxing and realizing that you have years to figure it out.

Willingness to Learn, Change and Grow

It takes work to have a great sex life. But maybe instead of seeing it as work, we should see it as an investment in our marriage! If we want to have a better sex life than we do now, we'll have to change. There is more to learn about sex—yes, even for you and me. Sometimes we act as if we know what we're doing, but how is that so if we never discuss these intimate issues with our spouse?

It sounds so simple—but if it were, people would have already improved their sex life. It's very sad that many people would rather stay frustrated, blame the other person or look elsewhere for satisfaction—which only leads to a whole new level of pain. Affairs begin, and marriages are destroyed. This is the irony: affairs take a lot of energy and creativity. If we invested that same energy and creativity into our marriage, it would make all the difference. As I (Philip) have sometimes said, "You can wander into an affair, but you can't wander into a great sexual relationship."

Selfishness is at the root of most marital challenges. Too often we don't look at how *we* might need to improve, or we don't look for opportunities for *us* to change, and instead we are frustrated at our spouse's behavior. Being willing to change and grow is essential to every part of a marriage, and especially in the area of sex. As we go through different seasons, our needs might change. What feels good might change. What we want might change. We need to be willing to change with each other.

I (Holly) read an article one time that described the top-10 things men want from their wives sexually. Rather than just implementing what I read, I asked Philip if he liked each of the things on the list. He was thrilled that I was reading an article like that and even more thrilled that I asked him if the list was true for him. Turns out that only about half of it was true for him.

And interestingly, his list has changed in the years since then.

Just when we get them figured out, needs change! Don't let this be frustrating; see it as an adventure. Just as in our relationship with God, intimacy is the goal, and it is more than technique; it is knowing the heart.

Tools for Great Sex

A Sense of Humor
The best way to break tension is to laugh. Not at each other or at the other person's attempts to please you but at the humorous situations that can arise. Relax. Playfulness is part of a great sex life.

Creativity and Imagination
Eating the same thing for dinner every night would quickly get boring, no matter how good it tasted. In the same way, our sex life can get a bit humdrum if we do not apply our God-given creativity to it.

In today's culture couples are encouraged to bring pornography via movies or the Internet into the bedroom. This is not the kind of creativity we mean. Bringing someone else into your bed, even if only in film, will eat away at the two of you working to become one.

But there are plenty of other ways to be creative. Turn on the music, and dance in the bedroom. Put on a sexy dress to catch his eye. Really, the ideas are endless. We are not going to tell you *how* to be creative, just that you need to be. And whatever ideas you come up with should be something both of you like and are comfortable with.

In his book *Love Life for Every Married Couple,* Ed Wheat writes,

I am suggesting that both husband and wife must use their imagination to fall in love, renew romantic love, or keep alive the *eros* love they now have. Remember that love must grow or die. Imagination is perhaps the strongest natural power we possess. It furthers the emotions in the same way that illustrations enlarge the impact of a book. It's as if we have movie screens in our minds, and we own the ability to throw pictures on the screen—whatever sort of pictures we choose. We can visualize thrilling, beautiful situations with our mates whenever we want to.

Try it. Select a moment of romantic feeling with your partner from the past, present or hoped for future. As you begin to think about that feeling, your imagination goes to work with visual pictures. Your imagination feeds your thoughts, strengthening them immeasurably; then your thoughts intensify your feelings. This is how it works. Imagination is a gift from the Creator to be used for good, to help accomplish His will in a hundred different ways. So build romantic love on your side of the marriage by thinking about your partner, concentrating on positive experiences and pleasures out of the past and then daydreaming, anticipating future pleasure with your mate. The frequency and intensity of these warm, erotic, tender thoughts about your partner, strengthened by the imagination factor, will govern your success in falling in love.

Of course this means that you may have to give up all outside attachments and daydreams about someone else if you have substituted another as the object of your affections. Many people who are not in love with their partner begin dreaming about someone else in an attempt to fill the emotional vacuum. Even if it is only in the fantasy stage, you need to forsake it and focus your thoughts on the one you married.[4]

The Right Atmosphere

You know that look women get when they want sex?
Me neither. —Drew Carey

Perhaps both men and women underestimate the importance of atmosphere, because atmosphere means something different to us both. Generally, men think intercourse, while women think kissing, touching, holding and hearing "I love you." The book of Song of Songs (sometimes called the Song of Solomon) should be required reading for all married couples. It starts with this line: "Kiss me—full on the mouth! Yes! For your love is better than wine" (Song of Sol. 1:2, *THE MESSAGE*). It's a good book! Each chapter is filled with ideas for creating an atmosphere of love and affection.

For most men sex could happen anywhere and be terrific; but for most women location is important. Atmosphere isn't just location, though location and timing are important. Privacy matters. Is the door locked? How bright is the light? Have you brushed your teeth? Where are the kids?

Atmosphere also has to do with the emotional climate, and while the emotional atmosphere tends to be more important to women, men are affected by it as well. In Song of Solomon, both the man and the woman are great at creating an atmosphere conducive to love. Words are a big part of creating this atmosphere. The couple in Song of Solomon compliments each other and creates a safe environment for each one to express needs and desires.

We've heard it said that foreplay is really just forethought; 95 percent of great sex is above the neck. If a man jumps into bed, pumps the gas and never turns the key, his wife lays there with a dead engine—and probably thinking, *What's wrong with me?* or *This did nothing for me. Why is sex such a big deal?*

The key is foreplay, and that means thinking of her first. If a woman enters into sex knowing that her husband's goal is to help her have an orgasm, she will be very interested rather than turned off. Men, focus on giving to your wife, and you will get back just what you want: an interested, passionate partner. It is easier to focus on what you want and what you need, but while it is important to communicate your needs, great sex occurs when we shift our focus from ourselves to meeting the needs of our spouse.

> Give, and it will be given to you. A good measure, pressed down, shaken together and running over, will be poured into your lap. For with the measure you use, it will be measured to you (Luke 6:38).

What words are you using to create an intimate atmosphere? Are you complimenting your spouse? Using loving words? You can begin creating the right atmosphere long before you even make it to the bedroom. In Song of Solomon, the man compliments his woman and loves her with his words long before he touches her.

In chapter 4 he begins by talking about her eyes, and then he compares her hair to a flock of goats. (I am assuming this is a good thing!) Then he talks about her teeth being washed and says that none are missing. (Good that none are missing, but you don't have to go into that same detail!) Next he mentions her beautiful lips, her temples and her neck. Later on in the book he comments that her nose is "like the tower of Lebanon" (7:4). (I am sure this was an awesome compliment, but I don't know if women of today generally want their noses referred to as towers.) And he looks at her waist and says that it "is a mound of wheat encircled by lilies" (7:2). (Again, I am sure that this is a lovely comparison for the woman he was talking to, but I imagine a woman of today would not be happy to have her waist and "a mound of wheat" mentioned in the same sentence.) He says that her breasts are as "twin fawns of a gazelle" (4:5), referring to their tender, delicate beauty. Are you getting the idea? All these words were spoken before he ever touched her. And I am sure that after hearing all these words, she was very ready to be loved.

Sometimes a man might say, "I'm just not a good talker." That might have been a good excuse when you were 13, but as a man, you need to get great at creating an atmosphere of love with your words. You don't need to refer to flocks of goats or twin fawns, but you need to get good at giving compliments.

Gentle, non-sexual touches also go a long way with women. Are you touching her during the day? Kissing her? Or are you looking for sex every time you touch her?

In an atmosphere of love, criticism will shut down the moment every single time. This is not the time to grab his love handles and squeeze or to comment about the 10 pounds she could lose.

Not every sexual encounter between the two of you will involve hours of time, music and candlelight. Sometimes it will be quick. "Quickie" often means that he has an orgasm and she doesn't, because it's pretty rare for a woman to have an orgasm in 30 seconds. She's not designed to. Quickies are fine occasionally, but they shouldn't be the only way you have intercourse. There needs to be a variety. Mix it up a little.

Shameless Sex

One of the most important ingredients in a great sexual relationship is an open attitude. "Adam and his wife were both naked, and they felt no shame" (Gen. 2:25).

Our desire is that you both enjoy the sexual side of your relationship without shame. We hope that the conversations started by this chapter will go a long way toward creating an even stronger bond in your marriage! Be honest and patient with each other. Relax. Have fun. Be creative. And enjoy the journey!

Think It Through

Women

1. Where did you get your information about sex? Was the information helpful, or was it something you had to overcome?
2. Are you comfortable talking with your husband about sex, about what you like and don't like? Have you gotten defensive about this instead of listening to him?
3. Are you faking your responses? If so, why? Why is it hard to be honest about what you need?
4. How many non-sexual touches did you give your husband today? Try more tomorrow!

Men

1. "Sex, which should be a gift to our life, will be a curse if it is not treated in the right way. While many people may not respect the biblical view of sex, our society's approach is not working." What do you think of these ideas?
2. As you go through different seasons in life, your needs might change. Are you talking with your wife about those changes?
3. How can you use your imagination to spice up your sex life? Spend some time this week brainstorming ways to make your love life with your wife sizzle.
4. What can you do to create a better atmosphere? What kind of foreplay does your wife expect and need? What words are you using to create an intimate atmosphere?
5. How many non-sexual touches did you give your wife today? Try more tomorrow!

Endnotes

Introduction: Thoughts from Philip
1. Judy Garland, "My Love Is Lost," from an unpublished collection of poems, 1939.

Chapter 1: Mirror, Mirror, on the Wall
1. "Without You" by Thomas Evans and Peter Ham, performed by Mariah Carey, *Music Box*, CD (New York: Columbia, 1993).

Chapter 2: Frog Kissing and Princess Rescuing
1. Gordon Livingston, M.D., *How to Love* (New York: Da Capo Lifelong, 2009), p. xiii.
2. Dr. Joyce Brothers in K. C. Baker, "The Kiss We Build Our Dreams On... New Research Shows Our First Smooch Is Our Strongest, Most Sensual Memory," *New York Daily News*, June 17, 1999. https://www.nydailynews.com/archives/lifestyle/kiss-build-dreams-new-research-shows-smooch-strongest-sensual-memory-article-1.839067 (accessed January 2014).
3. Livingston, *How to Love*, p. xxii.
4. C. E. Rollins, *Are We Compatible: Strategies for Making Your Personality and Background Differences Work for You—Not Against You* (Nashville: Thomas Nelson, 1995), p. 135.

Chapter 3: I Wish I May, I Wish I Might, Have a Great Marriage by Midnight
1. "Spirit of a Boy, Wisdom of a Man" by Trey Edwin Bruce and Glen Burtnick, performed by Randy Travis, *You and You Alone*, CD (Nashville: DreamWorks, 1998).
2. Henry Cloud and John Townsend, *Boundaries in Marriage* (Grand Rapids: Zondervan, 1999), p. 109.
3. "Diana, Princess of Wales: Engagement and Wedding," from Wikipedia. http://en.wikipedia.org/wiki/Diana,_Princess_of_Wales#Engagement_and_wedding (accessed January 2014).
4. Margaret K. Scarf, "The Remarriage Blueprint: Remarriage Is More Fragile than First Marriage," *Psychology Today*, January 12, 2009. http://www.psychologytoday.com/blog/the-bonus-years-adulthood/200901/remarriage-is-more-fragile-first-marriage (accessed January 2014).
5. John J. Ratey, M.D., *A User's Guide to the Brain: Perception, Attention, and the Four Theaters of the Brain* (New York: Vintage, 2002).
6. Dr. Robin L. Smith, *Lies at the Altar: The Truth About Great Marriages* (New York: Hyperion, 2007), pp. 159-183.
7. Sharen Pittman, "Divorce Hurts: What You Can Do to Avoid It," *Ezine Articles*. http://ezinearticles.com/?Divorce-Hurts—What-You-Can-Do-to-Avoid-It&id=2690665 (accessed January 2014).
8. Robert Grazian, "Statistics of Divorce," *Ezine Articles*, http://ezinearticles.com/?Statistics-of-Divorce&id=1468444 (accessed January 2014).
9. Jon Gottman and Nan Silver, *The Seven Principles for Making Marriage Work: A Practical Guide from the Country's Foremost Relationship Expert* (New York: Three Rivers, 2000), p. 4.

Chapter 4: The E5 Solution
1. Andrew Cherlin, *The Marriage-Go-Round: The State of Marriage and the Family in America Today* (New York: Vintage, 2010).
2. Nicholas Sparks, *The Notebook* (New York: Grand Central, 1999).

Chapter 5: Irreconcilable Differences
1. "Human Genome Project," Microsoft Encarta Online Encyclopedia, 2009. http://encarta.msn.com ©1997-2009 Microsoft Corporation.
2. LearnEnglishNow.com. *http://www.learnenglishnow.com/second_letter_is_u.html*, s.v. "cultivate."
3. Cloud and Townsend, *Boundaries in Marriage*, p. 164.
4. Renato M. E. Sabbatini, Ph.D., "Are There Differences between the Brains of Males and Females?" *Brain and Mind*. http://www.cerebromente.org.br/n11/mente/eisntein/cerebro-homens.html (accessed January 2014).
5. Christine Gorman, "Sizing Up the Sexes," *Time*, January 20, 1992. http://www.time.com/time/magazine/article/0,9171,974689,00.html (accessed January 2014).
6. Gary Chapman, *The 5 Love Languages: The Secret to Love that Lasts* (Chicago: Northfield, 2009).

Chapter 7: Sleeping with the Enemy
1. Anonymous, "The Too True Story of the Nail in the Fence." http://capitalogix.typepad.com/public/2012/07/the-too-true-story-of-the-nail-in-the-fence.html (accessed January 2014).
2. Smith, *Lies at the Altar*, p. 90.
3. Donald Clark, "Communication and Leadership," updated May 3, 2013. http://www.nwlink.com/~Donclark/leader/leadcom.html (accessed January 2014).

Chapter 9: Shift Happens
1. Linda J. Waite and Maggie Gallagher, *The Case for Marriage: Why Married People Are Happier, Healthier, and Better Off Financially* (New York: Doubleday, 2000), p. 148.

Chapter 10: Give Me Five!
1. Paul Reiser, *Couplehood* (New York: Bantam, 1994), p. 217.

Chapter 11: S-E-X Is Not a Four-Letter Word
1. "Trends in Reportable Sexually Transmitted Diseases in the United States, 2007," Centers for Disease Control and Prevention, updated January 13, 2009. http://www.cdc.gov/std/stats07/trends.htm (accessed January 2014).
2. "USA HIV & AIDS Statistics," *Avert*, February 2013. http://www.avert.org/usa-statistics.htm (accessed January 2014).
3. Armen Hareyan, "One-Third of Pregnancies in America Are Unwanted," EmaxHealth, May 10, 2007. http://www.emaxhealth.com/89/11909.html (accessed December 2009).
4. Ed Wheat, M.D., *Love Life for Every Married Couple* (Grand Rapids: Zondervan, 1980), p. 88.

Thanks to . . .

So many people who have helped us navigate our own marriage (some of whom we may never meet), including:

Gary Smalley, for helping us understand that our differences can make our marriage stronger,

Gary Chapman, for helping us speak each other's language,

Neil Clark Warren, for insights on people and on qualities to look for in a great mate,

Ashley, for reading through the initial manuscript so quickly and for correcting the typos and other glitches,

Our Oasis family, for wanting to learn about relationships and for being patient with us as we have taught about building them over the years,

And **Jordan and Paris**, our children, for keeping life exciting and love-filled.

Most of the time, we thank God for each other, and always, we thank Him for the privilege of being shepherds in His house.

GodChicks

For more information on the annual GodChicks Women's Conference,
Events & Media, please visit GodChicks.com

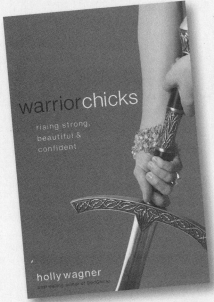